BECOMING AWARE . . .

A SERIES TO HELP JOURNEY THROUGH LIFE 101.

PUBLISHED BY:

PATTY KENNER

Dedicated to my guides and teachers with gratitude and love, and for all those searching for truth and meaning in life.

CONTENTS

PROLOGUE

It all started about nine years ago. I was sound asleep, and it was in the middle of the night. Suddenly, out of nowhere, these small pale blue lights began to appear. There were about four or five inches in diameter and formed small circles. They appeared first near my head and would gently flow over me in a line to my feet.

Now, this was not like seeing these with my physical eyes being open. My eyes were closed; I had been sound asleep! It was as if I was gently being awakened, but my eyes were still closed. They appeared almost behind my eyes.

I should preface this by saying that I have been meditating for over twenty years and have had some incredible experiences, but nothing like this!

At first, I did not really understand what it was or why they came, but over time I realized it was for the world to see for themselves, the truth of why we are here. I only hoped they were ready.

In reality, that was up to the individual soul. Me . . . I was just the messenger . . . and so it begins . . .

"What you are about to read begins a journey for each soul that searches for truth. The teachings of this book come from various realms in the universe. They are comprised from councils of highly evolved beings that are teachers, guides educators, and even those from the Angelic Realm. Yes, Angels are real!

They have been communicating with Patty over the last nine years. Their mission, their message, is to educate mankind and hopefully aid those on their journey through life on earth.

It is up to you, the individual, whether you discount these words or take them into your heart and soul. But we guarantee you one thing...once you read these words...you will never be the same in your thoughts, words or actions.

May the blessings of the Universe be will you always."

Council of All

The following transcriptions came to Patty on a personal level and helped prepare her for what was to come.

*****

'Thank you for being open to receive that which shall benefit the world. We shall discuss another venue for the soul's education.

We are known as the Trinity, the ALL. We do exist and have always existed within each individual soul as well as within the consciousness of the universe. Many speak of the Trinity as three separate states, yet again it is misrepresented. We may be seen as three, yet we are *One*, we are the *Whole*, we are the *All.*

There comes a point in every soul's development where our activation takes place. It takes many lifetimes for this to happen. As it occurs, it has a ripple effect on the energy grid. You may think of it as a sleeping molecule, always there, always present, yet only in sleep state until activation. Once activated, awakening takes place and a greater role is experienced.

The complexity of this understanding goes far beyond the perception of many souls. Therefore, we seek to simplify our explanation in order to be received on all levels.

Since the beginning of understanding and comprehension as you know it, there has been a great deal of deception and misrepresentation that has caused the continual increase of disruption in the matrix grid. All avenues and free will exist within the soul so that each must find their truth.

Picture the battle that exists within each soul, then magnify that on an infinite level. Also, picture the greatest level of dense energy you can imagine, going against the purest level of energy that can exist. This is our battle for ALL. That is why it is so vital for this information to spread far and wide. As it does, many who sleep in great darkness will slowly begin to awaken.

Please remember one's truth is always in a state of transformation. Your truth of today is not the same as yesterday. You evolve and transform each moment in time.

Once a soul begins to see, they start with baby steps before they can walk and run.

We honor you for your truth.

We are the "Trinity"

*****

"Blessings upon you. We wish to enter to establish our energy within you. We are the Tribunal Council of Thirteen which comes from the upper echelon of all that exists.

We speak to you about the anatomy of the soul. From the beginning of existence, there was only pure energy of love. Each soul came in pure and untarnished. Through thought and experience, that all changed and continues to disintegrate both individually and collectively. The ripple effect is massive.

It is the priority of each soul to return to this state of purity. This must occur for all. It is the way to redemption, the only means to succeed from reincarnation. Some souls, although finished, agree to continue existence on other dimensions in order to serve the Creator in any way possible.

It is the choice that is available for all. Some souls instead choose to work from this side. They delve into the darkest realms in order to help those souls that are stuck in the darkest realms of existences. This job, this action of love, is one of the most difficult of all. We call these *Warriors of the Light*.

These darkest levels have their own governing system. An agreement exists where these warriors are allowed to enter in order to help those with even the smallest spark of light.

Not everyone exists from this realm. There are those souls we call "the darkest of the dark energy", that cannot be reached. Although help is available, they choose not to accept it.

This concludes our topic for discussion at this time.

Blessings,

Council of 13"

*****

"Good evening. The blessings of the universe be with you.

When we began this project many years ago, you had no idea of what to expect. Yet you persevered through your doubt and as a result. The culmination will be present for all souls who seek inner truth and peace.

It is the totality of the soul which must be experienced. This means all parts of each and every soul must be integrated and healed in order to succeed from the wheel of reincarnation.

Through these teachings, that path may be eased a bit on the journey.

These teachings are not for the faint of heart, but for those determined to find their true selves. One must enter many realms to discover and face everything about themselves, their demons, their shortcomings, as well as their goodness and loving qualities. Each must be looked at as if through a microscope.

Truth must be found, and healing must take place. As this occurs, perceptions change, energy is transformed, and the illusion begins to dissipate.

What once was . . . is now seen through new eyes with clarity, understanding and wisdom . . . the soul has awakened.

Many will discount the words within these teachings. Let those fall by the wayside. The ones who see, the true warriors, will find them and reap the benefits.

Bless all those who dwell within these words and may the light of the Almighty Father flow through and around all mankind.

Namaste,

The ALL"

*****

The Beginning. Once upon a time, a new soul, a spark of light was born into existence on the earth plane. This soul was pure in heart and pure in energy.

As this soul grew and experienced everyday life, everything began to change. Their hearts learned through their feelings and emotions and their energy fields became impacted by all those souls who came in contact with them. The purity of heart became a jumble of confusion all because of the experience called life.

As the soul grew, it tried to make sense of the chaos and confusion. Where was the purity and peace that dwelled within? What happened that changed inside? How could it be found once again? What would it take to restore this inner peace?

These are all the experiences that each soul must travel on this journey of life. For some, souls are content to merely take each day as it comes, much like a hamster going around and around on a wheel.

Yet, for others, some event or experience marks a moment of change. It may be a life altering moment through illness, accident, loss or tragedy. Or it may be something simple such as gazing at the stars and wondering about life, their purpose, or destiny.

Whatever it is that calls deep within a soul; it is a turning point of change. It can be confusing on the outside, yet nothing could make more sense on the inside. Finally, the soul begins to awaken.

Life as they know it will never be the same. They are beginning to see with new clarity.

Generally, the exhilaration and excitement can barely be contained. They want to tell everyone, share it with the world and shout it from the rooftops! Some often try but are shocked at the results.

People look at them as strange, weird, or even crazy. Some wonder what has happened to them.

The world was just not ready for what they had to say. You see, it is the individual soul's journey; yet it is also the journey of all mankind.

Each must travel it alone before it becomes the collective. The collective is always there, always a part, yet it remains quiet, for now.

The soul has just discovered this journey begins on the inside first. And so it begins . . .

This concludes tonight's session. Many blessings of gratitude.

Council of 24

Enoch

*****

CHAPTER 1

Let us begin. The story of each soul is very diversified yet connected both individually and collectively.

Until a soul recognizes the universal connection, it is as if they are one small fish swimming in a goldfish bowl rather than being a part of and swimming in the ocean.

Picture the oceans of earth and each one being a universe. Somewhere you will find an avenue that will connect each of these oceans to each other. They are all part of the whole.

They each have their own individual names, yet whether by a stream or a trickle, you will find they run into each other and are connected. Each has its own character, yet also similarities.

The smallest body of water is the foundation. As it expands it develops similarities and characteristics of other bodies of water as well.

Soul connection, universal connection and multi-universal connection is like one small body of water being part of all other bodies as well.

Many souls choose not to consciously believe or understand the connection, while other souls have always felt or believed this connection exists.

As scientists expand their knowledge of the universe, the world and its eyes are forced open.

You are part of that expanded awareness. Your journey has just begun.

Blessings,

Council of 24

The information we bring forth is an effort to help humanity realize the implications and ramifications of their thoughts and actions.

Each soul's purpose is to embark on a journey through life in order to grow and develop in knowledge and maturity.

The soul on its initial step will be pure of heart. With each new incarnation, they have added many experiences and other soul's involvement in the process.

Sometimes these experiences mesh in balance and sometimes they clash. It all depends on the energy and thoughts of each soul and what they do with that energy.

The world, your world, the universe is love based. Yet, through the thoughts and actions of mankind, the love energy has been replaced by fear, anger and destruction.

Yes, the love is there, however, right now, it is buried under fear, hate and destruction.

How often have you seen a major catastrophe happen where the end result brings out people coming together to help each other through unconditional love?

Right now, there are many around the world devastated by what has happened in your election. Either way, whoever won, the people would have rebelled. Do you see that?

What matters from here on out is what is important. The world is watching, the universe is watching. It can be turned around and it won't be easy.

You are one of several we chose to act as a channel of love, a channel of hope, a channel of grace, honesty and redemption.

For now, you have merely a slight glimpse of the bigger picture. We realize there is a great deal to digest.

We shall conclude this session for now. We thank you for your service.

Council of 24

Hello and let us continue to discuss and educate. The nature of every soul is self-preservation both consciously and unconsciously. Each event or experience provides the opportunity not only for growth but to find one's truth.

Finding one's truth is seeking the Divine within self. Usually, only when one has exhausted the search for truth outside themselves, can they then begin to delve within themselves.

Truth will occur on many levels and have many faces. Sometimes, it is as subtle as a gentle raindrop or as loud as a bull raging through a china shop. It all depends on the soul level of growth, what can be seen, felt or heard, as well as what and how much they are willing to accept. Each is geared to the individual soul on whatever level is needed.

One also must realize that truth evolves. What one considers truth five years ago, or five minutes ago may not be the level of truth at this moment.

The more truth that is accepted, the more inner peace will exist. This comes as a result of experience, growth and generally a great deal of trial and tribulation, all of this being a result of divine design.

Divine truth will always prevail. Only the event and means of expression will change and transform. Each truth provides another gold brick on the road of life.

This concludes our discussion for today. Be at peace.

Council of 7

Good evening. Tonight's discussion will be on soul awakening.

When a soul reincarnates, in most circumstances, they enter with a veil over them. The thickness of the veil varies with the individual soul. This is done so that the experiences a soul encounters will not be influenced by their understanding of truth and wisdom.

A soul reincarnates for the purpose of soul development and growth. If they entered the earth plane with prior knowledge from past lifetimes, it would impact the choices and decisions they make through their experience. This way, their growth and development evolve, and is unencumbered by prior knowledge.

With that being said, there is also coding within each soul that is programmed to help lift the veil around them. Throughout a soul's timeline, various circumstances and events occur which are designed to help awaken each soul from darkness.

Some souls respond to the coding while others attempt to ignore it and continue to exist without the least bit of awakening. There are many factors involved such as time, the amount of coding used to lift and awaken the individual, etc.

The result is the same. Eventually, the soul will experience a lifting of the veil. To what degree, depends on the individual and their responses. For some, it may take eons of lifetimes, yet for others it may happen in a much shorter time. For the very elite, it can be done in one lifetime or in a moment of time.

This concludes tonight's discussion. More on this will come later.

Council of 12

Chapter 2

We are the world. What we think and say, we lend energy to and it can manifest. Once we learn that our reality comes as a result of thought, followed by action; then we can also realize we are choosing what we create.

Why do you think some people handle any situation in a positive manner while others see a similar situation and feed it only negativity? Choice, choice, choice!

Many souls come in to experience various situations. It is not the situation that is important; it's how we respond to that situation. Some will see themselves as being picked on, or a victim. Others will turn that same situation and learn from it.

Doing that changes the energy vibration of the thought, which changes the vibration of the situation. Sometimes, the change is small scale; other times there can be a greater impact.

All souls much learn from each experience. The more they learn, the greater the depth of understanding. A soul must seek to learn. Complacency will not suffice. Too much complacency will cause the soul a return ticket.

Once a lesson is learned and integrated, a new level of understanding takes place.

Always remember, thought is creation. Picture an individual thought of one and then picture the same thought of many. Imagine the power that exists behind it. That is why thought is so important. We are all responsible for our thoughts.

Council of 7

Today is about soul innocence. When a soul incarnates for the very first time, they exist of pure soul innocence. Each subsequent incarnation will have a degree of innocence. The amount of innocence is determined by the number of incarnations and the cell memories of unfinished lessons.

Each event, experience or unfinished lesson builds what we call soul clutter. This clutter can grow or diminish with each lifetime, depending on the choices one makes. As a soul grows in maturity and completes lessons, a degree of that innocence is realized. This comes from self-realization and detachment. As the process of detachment grows, truth and honesty are realized.

When this happens, part of the veil is lifted. Each choice of truth one makes expands their awareness. One of the biggest truths is realizing that each lifetime is about individual soul learning. It only plays a role with others when we take on a role either to pay our own karmic debt, or through agreement to aid another soul with their karmic debt.

When we have completed the cycle of reincarnation, any residual energy is removed and once again a soul returns home with a new-found innocence.

Search your world for innocence and you will find most innocence exists within a child, for they have the least soul clutter. The only clutter they have is what they brought into the particular incarnation.

Seeking truth can help achieve the innocence of a child. It is through being like a child that we enter the realms of heaven.

Blessings,

Council of 7

The dark may last for centuries. The evolution of the soul is a two-fold process. The first step involves the process of reincarnation. The second step involves re-entry into the spirit world. There are many areas within the two steps.

The individual soul is made up of many aspects. Each aspect must be realized and integrated before the soul returns to source.

Every lifetime experience is like the rung of a ladder; the higher you climb, the more of the soul energy is returned home. Even those souls who have passed to spirit world will have partial energy that still exists on other planes.

Only when the numbers are perfected is the soul set free and liberated. The lessons have been experienced and recognized.

We will continue the understanding of more next time.

I asked, "Who are you?" The answer came, "We are One in Seven".

The topic of today's discussion are expectations and vulnerability. Each situation a soul goes through has its own purpose. The biggest downfall occurs when we have expectations or desires as to how the experience will play out.

The energy of expectations can result in vulnerability. This happens when our expectations are not met, and the result was not what we wanted. This really is a control issue.

Just as we may try to control people; we try to control a particular situation and the outcome. Often, we don't like the result. When we can't control what happens, our vulnerability surfaces. Vulnerability is our insecurity rearing its head.

The truth is that if we remove the energy of expectations, we will find the situation often will end more favorably than we could have imagined. When we remove expectations, we gain personal power. Expectations also result from past lives. When we have expectations in an event or situation, it will replay itself until we learn what happens when trying to control the outcome.

Once we surrender, we remove expectations. The universe only wants each soul to live in peace and harmony with themselves and those around them. The only way suffering and despair enter the picture is by our own creation or through paying off karmic debt.

If we constantly worry about a situation, we will create the result of our energy. Energy follows thought.

Our surrender allows the universal energy to formulate the best result for all concerned. Without expectations, we are free. It is also another form of detachment.

Ponder these teachings. Look at areas of your life where you had expectations and the results. Then look at situations where you had no expectations and the result.

Expectations have their own power but only when we ourselves create and allow it. It is creation, however, usually we are not pleased with the outcome.

Surrender allows us the opportunity for peace and harmony. That is why we say it is an individual choice, so choose wisely.

Council of 7

Hello again. Today we continue with another discussion. Within your world exists the concept of free will. This is not present within the spirit realm.

Free will exists so that an individual soul may grow in learning and recognize the power of their own self through individual choice. They also eventually realize that there are consequences for each choice.

Many times, a soul will refuse to acknowledge their free will within a learning experience. Instead they seek to blame everyone involved within the experience for their demise. Yet this is where there free will exists. They are choosing to blame others for their choice, instead of another means of choice. This is sure to guarantee them continuous experiences of a similar nature. Each will offer them a different avenue of choice.

Only when they recognize the continuous pattern occurring, can they decide to try a different choice, therefore bringing a different outcome.

Here, on our realm, exists a flow of balance, yet within it are various levels. Lower levels here can only exist within the soul's reality, whereas higher levels of advanced souls exist with a more purity of balance.

Without self-balance, an elementary soul would have great difficulty trying to exist on a level of pure balance. Self-balance must exist first and again many levels present themselves all for growth and maturity.

An aware soul understands balance and seeks it always. They choose balance as they progress on each level. You often call it "drama", yet it is all merely imbalanced energy. Often souls choose to live in this energy because they think they benefit from it. Yet, the reality is they fear looking at what causes this thinking.

At various opportunities, a spark of balance can be shown to them, yet many are so fearful, they choose to return to their pattern of thinking because they believe it to be safe. They refuse to step out of the box and move forward. Thus, the drama continues.

Within each level are opportunities for growth by stepping outside the box. Again, it goes back to the individual soul and choice. It is the process of stepping outside the box and through one's fears. Think of all the various times this has occurred. Each of these choices brought new awareness and growth. Many lessons were learned and completed as a result, never to be seen again.

For a soul, the greatest discovery comes through self-examination. Remember, it all goes back to the individual as they continue the journey of awareness and growth. This concludes our teaching for now.

Peace,

Council of 24

CHAPTER 3

Good evening and the light and blessings of the Almighty One dwell in and around you always.

The journey of the soul both individual and collective is filled with caveats, confusion and misunderstandings. The personality, the human, can't begin to understand the true depth of the soul and what it must experience. It is, put simply, a matter of energies and transforming them.

This transforming of energy is what brings growth. When a soul is stuck, so to speak, in the same situations, repeating the same lessons over and over, it is merely because they refuse to see that the energy of the experience must be transformed.

Think about what happens when a soul repeats the same lesson over and over until one day they wake up, fed up and say, "I'm not doing this anymore. There must be a better way". In that moment, energy begins a shift and it is up to the soul how much is transformed and the amount of growth that can occur.

Until that moment of taking a stand occurs, the same lessons will continue to occur with different experiences. For many souls, these lessons can take many lifetimes and for others, they may seem to recognize the truth within the lesson very quickly. Each occurs in their own time.

Many souls want the understanding of others as a means of refusing to see what's inside themselves. It is the past which holds one back. Past experiences and refusing to forgive oneself and others are like chains to life and soul development.

Until a soul is ready to break those chains, they are held captive to the past. They may move across the country thinking they are creating change. It's true, they are creating physical change.

However, if the thoughts and energy of thoughts and behavior remain the same, they are still in chains.

Honor what you have accomplished; your chains are released. Do you see?

This concludes our lesson.

Blessings,

Council of 24

Good evening. It is good to be back in your energy once again. It is time to begin our transmissions and continue this journey.

In soul development it is the option of choice which can be affected by one's emotions and even one's intellect or reasoning. Each soul reflects on decision making skills differently. Yet, there are similarities as well.

Decisions are made from two avenues: the avenue of fear and the avenue of love. For example, a decision made by one soul who merely just wants to do the right thing no matter what, is based on fear. It may be fear of consequences, fear of judgment by others, fear or reprisal, just to name a few. In contrast, a soul who has grown in their development and is making a decision from their center of calm within themselves, makes that decision differently. They are not affected by external energies and emotions because their center of calm supersedes all else.

Think about decisions you've made in the past. Where do they come from? Even in the darkest day and the strongest difficulties, one must seek to operate from their center of peace. No person and no energy of interference should be able to affect one's center. That is the essence of peace within and there you will find love.

When one operates from this realm within, they own their choices. They own the power of their energy and their lives will never be the same. Please ponder and reflect on what has been said.

Blessings,

Council of 12

Thank you for this opportunity. Let us continue. Each individual soul has the opportunity to fulfill their destiny within each lifetime. As one incurs karmic debt, they also are provided the means within each lifetime to pay off the debt.

The turning point, or one major realization, comes when the soul understands that they are responsible for their own thoughts and actions. There is no one else to blame. It is never anyone else's fault; it is only found within the self-responsibility of the soul. Yet, to recognize and begin to be responsible often takes many, many lifetimes.

We are only responsible for our own thoughts and actions. When one discovers this truth, it goes a long way toward healing the soul. It is only through events and experiences that this can be found.

Karmic debt can be created quite easily. Simply treating another soul with intentional means of degradation or other means which lack compassion, may create karmic debt. However, if the role of that soul was to degrade another for a lesson to be learned or completed, there is no karmic debt. It is merely a well-played role or experience to help another soul.

The complexity of understanding karmic debt goes far beyond your realm. Many souls choose to experience a great deal of degradation in order to help balance the energy of mass consciousness. Often, the major events that occur result from the desire to help out in this way.

The light of this world is filled also with darkness. For change to occur, a great deal of events and circumstances must happen. Many times, it is through the greatest devastating circumstance that the most change takes place. We call these wakeup events for the soul. The events touch everyone on a soul level. Often, only when something major happens, do souls tend to come out of their particular state of trance. The destiny of your earth plane was designed to be a hypnotic state for each soul. The more experiences and lifetimes, the more soul impact.

A soul may choose to enter an incarnation that is filled with being of service to others. Yet, they give and give to others while never honoring or caring for themselves. Thus, balance cannot be obtained. One must first recognize their own importance. When they take care of themselves first, then they can properly care for others.

Mother Teresa is one prime example. Her life was filled with service, yet one only needs to be in her presence to recognize how greatly she honored her own soul.

Karla Faye Tucker is one soul who chose to effect change on a level of mass consciousness. She more than proved what change may occur within an individual soul. She impacted many other souls through her life.

For other souls, the impact may be subtler because they wish to remain in the background while still impacting the cosmos. Something as simple as paying for someone's layaway presents while remaining anonymous has an impact. It is one soul inspiring another soul all for the good of mankind.

Most souls have no idea the impact created on other souls. Often it is a simple gesture or word spoken that leaves a lifetime of impact or inspiration.

In the beginning to the end, it is all about the growth and maturity of the soul. The opportunities that exist have no boundaries. This concludes our discussion.

Be at peace,

Council of ALL

The lesson for today is gratitude. This emotion carries a good deal of weight. It is also a transformational energy.

When someone feels true gratitude, it changes the vibration of the energy all around them. It is like turning something sour into something sweet.

Each emotion carries its own level of vibration. The energy of gratitude carries one of the highest levels of vibration.

One becomes an alchemist when they can take energy from another emotion and turn it into gratitude.

We have previously talked about the importance of thoughts. Gratitude is one of the most valuable thoughts one can have.

Many souls don't even think about gratitude or what they have to be grateful for. It is such a major component within the grand scheme. Everyone has something to feel grateful for, no matter what their life situation may be, or how negative and disastrous it may seem.

There is always something to be grateful for. Maybe it might only start with waking up and a new day, or the sunshine, or a beautiful cloud. But that is a start that can change one's evolution of thought. It is a beginning.

Try making a list of gratitude for your life and you will be amazed at what you will find. True gratitude is life changing.

Often people are so caught up in daily life and what goes on around them that gratitude never enters a thought. It is such a shame.

As a soul begins to open in awareness and they see beyond the illusion; they start to find gratitude. Each moment of truth becomes a moment of gratitude.

True gratitude has an effect on a mass consciousness level. So, take a moment in your day and think of all the gratitude you have and its reason. You will find a great deal more than you realize.

This journey of life involves gratitude. Have gratitude for each moment in every situation you experience, each lesson, each triumph, each agony of defeat and you will learn far more than you could envision.

Watch the transformation of gratitude and see what happens.

Blessings,

Council of 7

CHAPTER 4

Today we wish to discuss more moments of soul awakening. For each soul, a moment of awakening may come in various degrees. For one soul it may come as softly as a quiet breeze upon one's face.

For another, it may come as though being hit by a huge boulder. Within each lifetime is the opportunity for awakening. It may be predestined prior to an incarnation or it may come as a result of an experience or choice made in that lifetime.

Many souls choose to have a particular point of awakening in a particular time frame, while others may leave it up to random happenings through experience.

As a result of free will within the earth plane, a soul still must choose to confirm or deny the awakening. Often a newly developing soul will choose to ignore or discard the experience out of fear or disbelief. They may think it comes within their imagination. When this occurs, another opportunity of greater depth will present itself.

For an advanced soul in development, the awakening merely comes as further growth and awareness.

There are a tremendous number of scenarios for this awakening to occur. For many souls, they wish to experience multiple different scenarios to discover exactly how, when and through what venue they were received.

It may take only the subtlest experience to provide an impact, or it may take what seems to be an explosion for an impact to occur. The circumstances are there; it is up to each soul to find them. For some it may take a near death experience for any major impact.

Once an awakening occurs it always carries great impact within the cell memory. This creates a foundation for growth which can be expanded within the life experience. It may be the simplest of experiences or the most difficult. The degree of difficulty will depend on each individual soul's choices.

Take some time to reflect and review this life's journey. Discover the areas and venues for soul awakening. Can you find the simplest of circumstances or was it a greater impact within an experience that was needed for awakening to be discovered? Journal what you discover. This concludes our discussion for today.

Blessings,

Council of 24

The time has come for another teaching. All that you are equals the whole of the universe. It is the separation that causes distress and disease.

The understanding one gains is through self-realization. It begins once you have removed your blinders to truth. Everyone who enters the earth plane has blinders. It is necessary for all. Individual truth and cosmic truth must be reached for the blinders to be removed. Each individual truth carries a ripple effect through the cosmos.

Some souls will remove a major number of blinders in one incarnation, while others must return again and again to remove a very small amount. It is a choice for each soul.

From this begins a new realm of understanding. Rejoice in it.

Council of 7

This lesson is about completeness. Each of us searches for it. We start outside of ourselves and will try anything to gain it. Sometimes we may grasp a tiny piece of it, but we can't hold onto it. Then we can't figure out how we got it in the first place.

Our wholeness comes when we totally accept all the parts of ourselves and embrace everything about us. It has nothing to do with anyone else. It is all about the individual and bringing the parts together.

We are all divided, or we wouldn't be here in the first place. Each time a part of that division is accepted and integrated, we are one step closer to completeness. Once we are totally complete, we have reached the end of this journey, #66. There is nothing left to complete. We have done it all. All that is left here is to live in the joy of our wholeness.

Council of 7

The teaching for today deals with being present in the moment. When a soul chooses to be present in the moment, he or she is aware of what's going on around them. Their energy is contained in that moment. When a soul is not present, their energy becomes scattered in a variety of manners.

If they are lending a thought to the past, that is where the direction of the energy is placed. If they are thinking of a future moment, their energy is directed there. Remember, energy follows thought.

Many souls live within the past or future. It actually creates an energy deficit. If emotions such as fear or worry are present, it can be destructive to the physical body. Operating at that level is draining to the soul's battery so to speak. It can cause a weakness in their energy field. This allows other energies to come in or a weakness of the physical body may occur. This also may lead to physical illness.

On a positive note, when a soul is involved in healing work from the past; it has a positive impact on the soul's energy. Anytime the energy of the past is released, that energy is retrieved into the soul body. Thus, the individual's level of well-being is increased. Nothing is greater than reclaiming one's energy and power. This helps create a solid energy field.

The positive impact will occur *as long as* the individual does not resurrect the past thought. If they choose to bring it forth again, then the past energy is actually reformatted. Once again, the draining of energy takes place. That is why being present is so important.

When you add emotions to these thoughts, it only magnifies the situation. All of this is Natural Law.

The more one stays in the present moment, the greater the impact. That is why monitoring your thoughts is so vital to soul growth. So . . . be present in this moment, just for today.

Council of 7

CHAPTER 5

Good morning. Once again, we are pleased to be with you. We offer these instructions as a means for souls to learn and be educated about the true meaning of life.

Each soul must discover their own meaning in their own way. There are always other souls who give aid where needed. However, the result must come from the individual soul.

Picture a wheel with many spokes coming from the center. The center represents the soul and the spokes represent the many lifetimes that must be experienced. Throw in free will, individual thought, and therein lies all opportunities for growth and truth.

Everything is energy, all thought, action, every molecule of life with each operating at a different frequency and vibration. Look at the energy of war and conflict; here you have a low vibration of energy.

Look at a group of monks secluded and meditating: The vibration is a much higher frequency. These are only examples of what exists in your realm. Add to that the density of the earth itself and you truly have a mass full of many opposite vibrations.

Within all this exists many souls, each on their own path, seeking to find themselves whether they consciously realize it or not. Each experience offers them the opportunity for insight.

Some souls experience a major event which causes the energetic change that begins their search. For others, it can be as simple as waking up and questioning the meaning of life, or simply realizing there must be more to life than the mundane in which they presently reside.

Whatever the cause, the meaning in their life will never be the same beyond this point. Thus, begins the search for peace and harmony both within and on the outside.

They must weather all hurdles and obstacles along the way. Once found, this true peace and harmony survives beyond all. Some souls may experience it for a brief moment, while others may reach for the nirvana inside. It is the truth of all, existing within *The All*. Words become inadequate to explain or describe it. It is heaven within.

When a soul reaches this aspect of self, a transformation occurs. Remember, it is merely energy returning to the *source of ALL*. It was always present within the soul. It was only covered by the layers of lifetimes yet to be discovered.

Council of 7

Good evening and thank you. Tonight, we wish to provide education once again for humanity on soul development.

We shall speak on soul awakening. The specifics for each soul's opportunity to awaken varies, yet there are main characteristics that are similar in nature.

Each soul has three general opportunities to awaken within an incarnation. Beyond this point, it may vary according to the choice made by the soul. Some souls are so affected by the experience, that they immediately begin the moment of awakening as if someone has rousted them from a deep sleep. They feel an energy shift deep within their soul.

Another soul having a similar experience tries to minimize or discount the experience through their thoughts. They can even take it to the point where they question whether it really ever happened.

An example might be a soul who drives too fast and reckless, almost ending in a severe head-on collision. Yet, at the very last moment, the collision does not occur. At first, the soul thinks, "There is no way I avoided being hit", and even slows his driving habits. Yet, the more he thinks about it, the more he discounts it until he talks himself into believing it did not really happen. He goes right back to his old driving habits.

For this soul, a different type of experience will occur in order to get his attention.

Within the incarnation, a soul must make the choice to change in thought, behavior and action. For some souls, it may be gradual. For example, a soul may realize there is more to their life than what they see each and every day. They begin to search within themselves through books, meditation and other means. They feel as if their soul is being fed.

Then, there is the soul who has an experience that begins to open their eyes, yet they take a wait and see attitude. They feel the effect of what they experienced, yet they want proof that is real and can be experienced again. These can be more difficult because they place terms on how or what shall be provided for it to satisfy their truth meter.

An example would be someone who has had a true spiritual encounter yet asks for it again while placing demands or a "show me this" specifics. If it is not provided, they may discount the experience all together.

Nothing is by coincidence, yet many believe it is. Each experience with another soul provides the opportunity to awaken from the darkness or sleep. It may range from miniscule to cataclysmic. One never knows the impact they may have on another soul through their actions or words.

Now, be aware of your encounters each day and seek to help another soul to awaken.

Blessings,

Council of 13

Good day. Today our discussion involves around energetic disruptions and their effect on the soul and its physical body.

Each individual is exposed to many varieties of disruption. A soul's energy can be relatively smooth until they walk into an area of mass energy that is disruptive. It may be energy of a lower vibration and have the makeup of lower emotion. When a soul is open and walks into this energy, it changes the vibration around them and even through them.

Another soul, who guards and protects their own energetic field, can walk into that same lower field of energy with little or no effect. Thus, the importance of recognizing and protecting your field of energy.

Any soul seeking to grow in maturity and development will find this same disruption. They may not understand why they can walk through a crowded area and soon feel drained of energy or feel irritable. They can't figure out why. The longer the experience, the greater the impact.

Think about the places where your energy field is openly exposed in your day and please draw it in for protection. It will go a long way in helping you. This concludes our lesson for today.

Council of 24

CHAPTER 6

The purpose of these teachings is to have the capacity to provide wisdom, knowledge and education that will reach a multitude of souls.

Many of the teachings are elementary in nature and many are designed on a much deeper level. Yet, each teaching will reach every soul on many levels. Today we continue with another lesson.

As a soul advances both in maturity as well as in their age, many changes begin to occur. A point is reached within each lifetime where a process of withdrawal begins to take place. Some souls simply withdrawal energetically from their surroundings. As this happens, the energy is transferred to the spirit world. The soul slowly begins to return home.

For some, it is a simple process, yet for others, there may be a struggle. The soul decides the timing and can even delay or expedite the process. If a soul feels the lifetime and what was designed to be completed has been accomplished, it may be expedited. A soul at peace leaves simply and easily.

A soul whose death is extremely sudden or unexpected to those on the earth plane, is merely a designed plan. Often the plan is created for the growth and development of others and or to raise the consciousness of the masses. Each departure and design has its own merits.

Also, depending on the awareness of the soul, the experience will differ greatly. Some souls require a great deal of healing if they have experienced a long physical or mental illness.

Others may require a great deal of counseling and orientation to their surroundings. Whatever each individual soul needs is provided.

Usually, the most challenging occurs when an individual's belief system regarding the death process is based on fear. Fear exists as a complete block to light and must be eliminated before one can truly progress.

Often, it is far easier to educate a soul who thought they were an atheist, rather than one who simply and totally fears death. Atheists merely need proof to believe. Those who exist in fear are a different story.

That is why we talk of planting seeds. For those who have been misinformed through religion, merely planting a seed of true wisdom will cause enough light to expand throughout their being.

One may think they believe their religion, because they follow the masses. Then, put them outside that environment in a discussion with a soul providing truth and all of a sudden, they have beliefs to contemplate. Thus, a seed is planted. From that point others will come along to feed and nurture. As a result, by the time the death process occurs, they are on a different level of belief.

It is only through the chaos of the masses that fear is produced. The more truth that is recognized, the more growth can occur.

Blessings,

Enoch

Good day. We wish to continue the lessons. We will discuss the avenue through which one soul may discover self-understanding. There are many means for this to occur.

Often the easiest means of discovery comes through another soul. Picture each soul who incarnates having a blueprint for the incarnation. The blue-print is a map of experiences, crossroads and decisions for that soul. In order for synchronicity to occur, the involvement of many other souls must be present.

Remember, each soul has their own blueprint and still each blueprint is part of a universal blueprint. The entire process is magnanimous.

Self-discovery can occur simply through the experience of another soul. In order for this to happen, the soul must be receptive to the process. Often times, this is not the case. Many times, the ego will interfere so that any means of learning is discarded. Again, it is an individual choice.

Simply put, some souls are so encased within their own density of life; they have no wish to evolve or change. They merely seek to go through the repetitive motions of day to day life. Unless they choose to break out or some experience rattles their cage, nothing will happen until their life is reviewed. Every soul must experience this level. For any soul seeking to grow, self-discovery will present itself.

Self-discovery comes through dream state as an avenue as well. The ego may try to intervene. However, when one utilizes the dreams as a means for growth, self-discovery will eventually prevail.

Within each blueprint are many areas for growth. Each must consist of physical, mental, emotional, and spiritual components. Picture the inner workings of a clock. If one small piece is not in sync, it affects the entire clock.

Each blueprint is the map for each incarnation of a soul. The goal is synchronicity of the blueprint. When it or a part of it is out of sync, this merely provides the means of a new blueprint for rein-carnation.

For the wheel of reincarnation to be completed, each blueprint for each lifetime must be in sync with the universal blueprint. Only then has a soul completed this wheel. Please ponder this message and all it entails.

Council of 24

This universal teaching will seek to expand the awareness of the passing of time as you know it. There is difficulty for a soul embedded within the earths dense energy to understand the time-space continuum.

Although each world has its own energy of existence, there also is a revolving continuum of space. From your world, it is difficult for many to understand all energy is connected and the moving of energy in all worlds occurs at the same moment of existence. Everything is happening together.

For anything to manifest within your realm, it must occur on our higher planes first. Only then can it manifest in your world. From your time-space perception, the denser the energy of the world, the longer it takes to manifest.

Picture an event happening and being seen on both your east coast and west coast at the same time. Yet, there is a three-hour time difference. It still happens at the same time.

As these simple exercises begin to take on an understanding, more questions begin to surface. As a seeking soul begins to question, the answers will come. It is only when one is open to receive that this can happen.

Remember when you were thinking inside the box? Then you stepped outside the box in thinking; yet you were still trying to live and think inside and outside at the same time. You then reached a point where you could not do both. So, you stepped completely outside the box. Once there, you realized that all the thinking inside the box no longer made any sense at all. This came because you expanded all your awareness on a universal level. The more of this that occurs, the greater the awareness received.

As a soul completes the numbers necessary, their soul eye becomes acute. When this happens, there is a splitting that begins to take place. Their awareness begins to shift from the physical to the spiritual on an energetic level.

Picture a kite that is being flown for the first time. As it catches the first wind it begins to take off. It is bumpy and jerky at first. The kite may even hit the ground before taking off again. Yet, once its under enough air, it soars to great heights.

Now, picture the line that tethers it to the physical, being cut or released. This exemplifies the soul experience of release. For some, it may take a longer period than others. It is the freedom within the soul that sets them free.

When a soul is free in mind awareness on a spiritual level, they cut the string that tethers them to the physical. Regard each experience that occurs as an opportunity on all levels of learning. Search your heart and soul to find the meaning of each experience. Be especially aware of the intentions of others and you will learn a great deal.

Peace is at hand,

Council of 24

CHAPTER 7

Tonight, the lights came in the form of a white light in the shape of a triangle, that then flowed into a cross.

Good evening. May the blessings of the Universe be yours.

We come to speak to you about the unity of the soul. All parts, all aspects of one's soul, must be unified both to itself and the whole. There must not be any division, no cracks, or disturbances within the energy of the soul membrane. The goal of every soul is complete unity of self and of the whole.

Right now, one sees the devastation, the chaos and destruction in society. This is not unity in any way shape or form.

Each individual soul must seek the unity and peace within the core being first. Until that is complete, the unity of the world is not possible.

All must start within the self. It all begins with you. Each soul must have the core of peace and unity.

We thank you for this time.

THE ALL

Tonight, when the lights came in, they formed pale blue triangles that appeared and flowed in a line.

Good evening. Let us begin. Each and every soul must find their path to awakening. There are many avenues for this to happen.

For some souls, the experience occurs once in a while, over various lifetimes. For other souls, the event for awakening occurs in each and every lifetime. When this happens, it increases their soul growth and development to a greater degree.

Each is predestined and designed by the soul. Some would rather take their time; others seem to want it all at once.

Although the experience to awaken presents itself, it still is up to the soul whether and how they respond to the event. Some may even ignore it. Others respond immediately as if they were hit with a ton of bricks. Their lives are never the same.

For the soul who ignores or minimizes it, they continue their behavior until another event occurs, whether in the same lifetime or another.

Do you see why the role of free will plays such an important part? The dynamics of free will is so understated. It forms many major disruptions both in society and the world.

Just think about the issues going on in the world on a day to day basis. These issues are the result of free will, choice and the lack of responsibility when making those choices.

Choices which impact the world energetically are hastily made without thinking through to the consequences. It is much easier to blame others than assume responsibility.

Now, do you see why we stress the importance of thoughts, energy and consequences? The results can be catastrophic.

You can now begin to understand Natural Law and why free will, as you know it, does not exist here on our realms. More on this will be discussed later.

Blessings,

Council of 24

The teachings of the soul are all encompassing. It is necessary to break these into segments. It also gives you time to digest it all. There is a universal code that exists within each soul. It is a master programming of it all. This also includes past incarnations.

Some souls will have a great deal of programming that will be activated within an incarnation. Others may only have a small amount activated. It depends on the maturity of the soul and choices they made.

All programming is done through the matrix of numbers. There will come a day when souls entering a new incarnation will have conscious awareness of this code. It will depend on the degree of veil that is lifted. Also, it will take a very long time for that to occur.

Right now, you will hear of various individuals in child state that have knowledge of their past lives. There was no need to search for them; they spoke of them as soon as their verbal skills were apparent. Others have genius traits of specific knowledge above all those on earth.

All of this is the result of programming. As the vibration of the earth increases, many similar happenings will occur. We are talking about the increased vibration in collective consciousness.

Just as this programming will rise; you will see strangers, so to speak, that will bring forth master teachings for all. This too occurs through programming.

There are many other avenues here that we will explore at a later time. That is enough for now.

Council of 12

CHAPTER 8

Good evening. Let us continue the story of the soul and its journey. When an event occurs where the soul begins to awaken, changes develop physically, emotionally, and spiritually. This occurs both internally and externally.

It is eventually noticed by others even though they do not understand and can't put their finger on what has changed. It often provides a state of confusion both for the soul and others around them.

For some, it can be frightening, for others, just confusing. They don't understand what has changed or why it has happened. From an energetic viewpoint, each soul has their own blueprint and that blueprint is connected to a part of the universal blueprint.

As the change occurs, the coding within the blueprint is changed through activation. Picture a blueprint of dots on a grid. As the activation takes place, the dots begin to light up, not all at once, but a few at a time.

As soul development continues to grow, a greater understanding is realized. It is in that moment a part of this grid is connected. In other words, before these lighted dots may have been spread apart on the grid. At the moment of realization or understanding, the lighted dots are connected and become a quadrant. This occurs on a soul level. Remember the quadrant.

This shall suffice for tonight's teaching.

Blessings,

Council of 12

Good evening. Let us begin.

The evolution of the soul takes place on many dimensions all at the same time. From its inception, the energy of the soul exists everywhere. It is both individual and collective energy all rolled into one.

As soul growth takes place, wisdom, knowledge and understanding expand. This energy, no matter how small or large, affects the whole. Think of it as the ripple effect. Energy of one affects the energy of those around that one.

Think of a person who enters your awareness. They are angry and the minute they touch your energy field, you feel their anger. Your own energy field contracts as a means of protection. Someone else enters your awareness. They are peaceful and happy. When this soul enters your energy field, you feel their joy. Your energy field expands in union. This too has a ripple effect.

These are two very simple examples of how energy affects both the individual and the collective.

The natural disasters that have occurred recently are having major effects on both the individual soul and the collective energy of the whole.

We must work together to seek the balance through Natural Law. It is the balance of all things, all energy. It is about the individual soul finding balance first within themselves. When one soul attains balance, within them, within their core, it benefits all.

Seek your balance. It is necessary for peace both within and without. Align yourself through the Laws of Nature. You will find it of great benefit.

The ALL

Good evening. Tonight, begins a new realm of awareness and teaching.

As a soul gains knowledge and wisdom, so does the amount of responsibility increase. Their world as they know it, begins to change. Old ways, old thoughts and patterns no longer work.

As realization begins, so do changes in thought and behavior. Old thoughts and patterns may try to creep back in, but they must be nipped at the onset. Otherwise, a soul will find themselves taking steps backward instead of forward.

There are always energy forms that will try to discourage a soul on their journey. It is through these lessons where a soul learns the greatest. Each path is different, yet each is the same.

A soul must gain strength, determination, and fortitude from within. This is growth, this is wisdom and knowledge. This is the path, the journey of the soul.

Blessings,

Council of 24

Tonight, the blue lights came in different shapes, all flowing one on top of the other, then fading away.

Good evening. Tonight, we shall discuss the continued evolution of the soul. When a soul has an event or experience of awakening, whether large or small, it has a major impact.

Upon first instinct, many choose to ignore the impact or even to question whether it even happened. Others may immediately dive in and want to know everything. Yet, still others may seek to know more, but are fearful at the same time because of what is unknown. They may even take a "wait and see" attitude.

Still, in each of these scenarios, change begins to occur both within and around them. They feel it, others see it and yet no one may be able to explain it. All they know is something happened.

From here, some souls continue going back and forth between their life of what was and the life as it stands presently. These two dichotomies continue to clash until the soul realizes they can no longer continue in this manner. This is a major turning point.

Many souls must step away from former lives as they knew them for something so foreign and unknown. It is only in the depths of the soul that knows they can't go back.

It's like fitting round pegs into square holes. Their lives will never be the same. It may be exciting for some, while others are frightened beyond anything they have experienced.

It is here during this phase when a great deal of education occurs during dream state. This happens on a soul level and the individual is usually blocked from bringing it back to the conscious state. More is accomplished this way than any conscious education or development.

The energy resonates within the depths of the soul and filters outward. Here is where a large amount of coding is programmed and activated at the proper time. Often it is referred to as an "Ah ha moment". Yet the reality is that it is merely divine coding, timing and activation.

This concludes our session.

Blessings,

Council of All

The value of this lesson comes from deep within the soul. All that we become is a result of our past lives and past experience. From the moment the soul begins its first journey, it is in a state of perfection.

As they begin their growth, each is affected in different ways in the experiences of life. Two souls can have the same exact experience and have two completely different responses or reactions. Why is that?

The reason may deal with several options. First, what lessons has the soul come in to learn and experience? There is a great deal of planning and execution in order to help another individual soul or even themselves. As each event is experienced and the learning is processed, then the difficulty of each lesson will increase. It is the way in which the greatest learning can take place. The density of the earth plane allows this to occur.

For a soul to move to a different level, they must have repaid any karma and also have accumulated the correct numbers for completion to happen. There can be completion on many levels and often takes many lifetimes.

The amount of lessons learned is decided by the individual soul and is obtained through counsel with many masters within a the universe. In an extremely high level, a soul is allowed to make the choice themselves, but most souls need the universal council that is available. It involves their level of maturity in soul growth.

Also, a soul will often try to overload themselves to have greater completion. When the choices are made in the energy of the universe, it seems easier to tackle a great deal. Then, when the soul enters the density of the earth plane, they begin to realize the difficulty of what they hoped to accomplish. In some cases, their plan may be altered.

On another occasion, a soul may only choose to go through a minimal amount of lessons. Yet, once they enter that particular lifetime, they continue to go above and beyond what they had decided to complete. It is accomplished all through their experiences.

You must remember that lessons learned occur on many levels: physical, mental, emotional and spiritual. Each area must be completed. Sometimes the soul will complete it on one level and think they have finished. The reality is that they must repeat a similar experience to finish all levels. That is why you may hear someone say, "I'm so glad I finished that lesson", when they may have only completed a piece of it.

Help, in any form, is available for all who may seek it. They need only to ask. Stubbornness is often the culprit which prevents many resolutions from occurring only because they have failed to ask. It is often an, "I can do it myself" attitude. Just think of this ... if a soul cannot ask a neighbor or friend for help, how can they ask the universe for help? It is as simple as that.

Each soul has their own lessons, as well as frailties to work through. Many lessons must be learned through the higher levels of the heart instead of through the emotions. For many, this is where the difficulty occurs. When they work through the lower levels of the heart, it can be more difficult to transform to the higher levels. It is easier when one is working through the intellect, to move it into the proper area of the heart.

If one is in the lower emotions, often stubbornness is an element that has to be overcome before the lower emotions can be transformed. Please ponder all that has been given in this lesson.

Council of 12

CHAPTER 9

The purity of a soul's heart is measured by its actions, all actions.

Have you ever noticed two children playing? Then a moment later they are fighting. If may be a simple act of one taking the other's toy. Sometimes, it may escalate to a shoving match. Other times, with merely a simple apology, they are once again friends, all is forgiven and forgotten.

Then, as a soul goes through life experiences, they become aware of the external influences of others and their surroundings. With each experience, they become incrementally aware of the results of their choices and the resulting consequences.

All souls must experience the gamut of trials and tribulations. That is called growth development. Some try to do it all in one lifetime, while others spread it out slowly life after life. Yet, all must be experienced for development.

The challenge within a soul lies in how they respond to these experiences and then it is a choice. One soul, having experienced sorrow, tragedy, and the like, along with joy and happiness, may choose to rise above the sorrows, focus on the joys and turn it into helping others. This is being of service to all mankind.

Another soul, having the exact same experiences chooses to wallow in their misery, blame others for their misfortune and take on a victim role. Again, it is a choice. Merely look around you and you can see it in their eyes and their actions. Even those who are wallowing are always given further experiences which could offer a different response in choice.

Many times, a soul must reach a breaking point before they choose differently. Yet, all it takes is that one different choice to change the energy around them. Only they are responsible for their choices, no one else. And so . . . it begins in increments.

For some, it happens in baby steps. For others, it can be in leaps and bounds. Yet, each increment offers a turning point in a soul's life. Reflection aids the process. It is not so much delving into the past as it is seeing the point where a soul made a different choice. The hamster gets off the wheel and no longer goes around and around.

From this point a soul's eyes begin to see more clearly. They watch and observe what goes on around them. Thus, begins a leap in self-awareness. Every step is like the run on a ladder. The more steps they take, the higher they go on the ladder. The result of shifting energy occurs both inside and outside of the soul. It impacts not only them, but others who come in contact with them.

Others won't understand it, but they do feel it. Sometimes a simple act can be the catalyst for another soul without them even knowing it. This is why we stress the importance of each encounter with another soul. You never know where it's going or the impact it may have on others.

Choices and their consequences are a gift on this journey of life. Use them wisely.

Blessings,

Council of 24

Today we honor the presence within you. Within each soul is the eternal spark. This flame shines in all souls. It is up to the individual soul as to the amount of growth in each lifetime. A variety of development may be chosen.

A difficult lifetime with a great deal of turmoil in experience may be chosen in order to pay off karma or even to help aid another soul in advancement. Each plays a role, and each learns through experience.

The more maturity of the soul, often the more challenging the lifetime. When a soul chooses a long or debilitating illness, it is for the benefit of many besides the individual at hand.

As a soul's numbers are completed, there is a shift in their energy. As this shift occurs, more soul energy starts to return to source. The more that is completed in numbers, the greater the percentage of soul energy returned.

This only begins when a soul has reached a point where the greater parts of their numbers have been fulfilled. This happens when a soul recognizes their energy and soul aspects, as well as when their journey is nearly completed. The more energy that is returned prior to their actual exit, the easier the transition. This may happen through illness, through coma, or it can occur gradually in an advanced soul state.

You will experience the energy returning to the source. It will feel as though *a part of you is leaving*, which is exactly what is happening.

We describe part of what occurs on the journey so that others will benefit from the experience. This will help dissipate the falsehood of information that is presented elsewhere. We provide truth. The teaching comes long before the experience. This truth will plant seeds within those who are exposed to it. It provides the greatest opening for all.

Within the world's turmoil, peace will be found. Please know that all events in the state of your plane are necessary and part of the design plan. Though misunderstood in your world; it has complete understanding in ours.

The world is exactly as it should be. Remember this and understand its meaning goes far beyond what you see and experience.

This concludes the information for today. Follow your heart to find peace.

Council of 24

It is the nature of the soul to identify all aspects within the individual personality. Some souls have chosen to take on more than one personality, thus, the need to identify and integrate many aspects. This can be a great challenge for the soul, but once again it is a choice.

If a large mirror was placed in front of you, you would see the image of yourself. But there would actually be two images; the one you see reflected back at you through the mirror and the one which is the true soul.

What you see in the mirror is only your perception, not necessarily the truth. If one person stood in front of the mirror and ten others stood around the mirror, you would have ten different perceptions of what they saw. It is much like the story of the elephant.

As we grow in conscious awareness, our perceptions change. When this happens, more truth enters the consciousness. Truth overrides perception.

Council of 7

This teaching will be about violence. Violence carries its own energy. It also carries an impact on a mass consciousness level. It can feed on itself. Violence is comprised of dark energy.

To an individual soul, this energy may seem to have a life of its own. It carries a lower vibration when it is active. It is also relative to the amount of negative energy in and around an individual.

If an individual does nothing to try to raise their vibration, the negative energy will have more impact. Negative energy begets negative energy and positive energy begets positive energy.

Karma also may play an influential part. If a person must experience the negative energy in an event due to karma, then it will happen.

Please also remember that with Universal Law, balance must occur. At times a negative uprising may be planned so that change can occur on a mass consciousness level. There is always a positive spark within a negative and a negative spark within a positive.

Many times, the largest of negative experiences will have the greatest positive impact on an individual or mass consciousness level.

All you need to do is look at major world events to see the repercussions both positive and negative. A short impact of negative energy may also have a longer positive impact.

Remember, we all come in here to play a role in the grand scheme. Some come in merely to play an extremely negative role in order to have a greater positive outcome. It may also be to balance their own karmic debt, or to help someone balance their debt. You must look at Universal Law when looking at all that happens.

The vibration of this plane itself is all a result of Universal Law. Each event or experience has a purpose. For an individual, it is not what it may seem to be.

Universal Law must be taken into account in order to understand it. Only then can truth be revealed.

Take some time to look at the Universal Laws and we will bring in more understanding and enlightenment over the weeks to come.

Blessings,

Council of 7

We continue our lessons. The ability of the soul to recognize and acknowledge its aspects depends on various factors.

Most often the deciding factor is the soul's individual development level. However, another strong factor involves the collective consciousness.

All information is stored within the universal consciousness. Therefore, it is always readily available to all. When the individual is aware and recognizes the unconsciousness, then it is as if the lid was taken off a metal can. The world opens up to us. Yet, for many, this unconsciousness understanding is not present. It may take lifetimes to have this understanding. As you well know, a soul developing can be experienced in thousands of ways.

They may be on a spiritual path of their own yet be totally unaware of the collective consciousness. However, the collective consciousness is always connected to each soul. They merely have not brought it through to a conscious state.

Picture a basket filled with eggs from all different animals. To one soul, it is merely a basket full of eggs. Yet, to another soul, they are aware of each egg, it's entire makeup and everything about it.

All knowledge is available to all souls. It is up to the individual soul to aim for that knowledge and understanding. This means challenging everything in their belief system. It is thinking outside the box so to speak. For many this can be frightening. It is this challenge which opens the way to the greatest development.

Other times it is a tug of war within the soul as they have existed within a belief system, which is now being challenged. Nothing is the same. Once they begin to see what a major role their thinking and beliefs have, the challenge begins. When they see and understanding the thinking inside the box, then they can alter or change that thinking.

The challenge comes when they are thinking outside the box while still trying to exist within the box. Then they find the conflict, and it no longer works. They can't do both. They still will try but it just no longer works. The challenge comes through existing still with those in the box, while still being outside the box. It involves the greatest conflict of all. Just imagine how many different systems of thought exist within the collective consciousness.

For some, a change in thinking may occur easily, while for others it is a long, ongoing struggle. It may be an explosion in thought or just merely a small spark. It all happens in vastly different ways, yet this spark was what was needed for that particular soul.

Several factors must be realized. One, the misinformation that is being taught can be destructive. That is why the veil must be lifted.

Many are chosen to serve and while they may think they serve the universe; they are often serving their own ego. They glamorize what they think is knowledge and understanding when it is not truth.

There is only one path. Still, there are many avenues along this path.

Along the journey disciples are present. They offer truth. Many are not ready for that truth.

In time the masses will be reached. This will open the eyes of many who cannot see. This is the journey, the destiny.

Be at peace.

Council of 24

Good day. Today we shall expand on some previous discussions.

We have mentioned that a soul endeavors to clear up various un-learned lessons with each incarnation. We also have discussed how other souls will give aid where needed to help dissolve their lessons.

One must constantly remember that an incarnation is like a major play appearing on a stage. Consider the title as being one lesson for one or more souls. Each actor has their own role to play. As with all roles, some are villains, and some are heroes, with the rest falling somewhere in the middle.

As each act occurs within the play, many changes take place along with many variables at hand. Of course, free will is involved. The hope is that through various scenes and actions, soul growth and advancement will occur within the lesson. Often this is the case, but often it is not.

The best scenario happens when a soul is searching for answers within themselves. They have reached a point of questioning the mundane in their life. Herein will their eyes begin to open within a play, and true soul growth occurs.

However, on the opposite end of the spectrum is a soul completely embedded within the mundane and outside themselves. Maybe their role is that of a villain. The more opportunities that exist, the deeper they go within the role. They see themselves as being per-secuted and toot the images, *Life is unfair or it's not my fault.* A soul who is unwilling to take responsibility for their thoughts and ac-tions merely becomes a soul stuck on a wheel that goes around and around, the wheel of reincarnation.

Only when this type of soul experiences an earth-shattering event, can they begin to change. Often it takes eons of lifetimes.

For every soul, it is about what they experience, and the choices involved. In order to complete this wheel., all must be in complete and total balance.

This is what the soul within you, this author, has experienced. Through many lifetimes, you have reached your nirvana. You see with eyes open in a way you have never experienced before. You watch various lessons unfold, speaking when its valuable, while remaining silent when it is not.

You have reached non-judgement both of others as well as yourself. You wish only to help others who may be struggling and searching for meaning in life. We honor all you have done in the name of service. We honor you. This is available for all who are searching. Good day.

Council of 7

CHAPTER 10

Thank you for taking this opportunity to expand the energies of our teaching. We only have a few more instructions to complete this segment of our endeavor.

For a soul to complete its journey through reincarnation, all of its energy must be in balance. This brings up another misconception. Often utilized through the means of the Bible, is the passage referring to what is thought to be marriage. It speaks the words, "and the two shall become one". Religious teachings deliver a message which could not be further from truth.

It speaks not of the physical man and woman joined to become one. The truth is the balance of the masculine and feminine aspects of the soul being in complete and total balance, joined together as one. Remember, it is not about physical bodies; it is all about the energy of the soul.

It takes many lifetimes for this balance to occur. We have simplified our explanation, in order for the deepest understanding to occur.

Now, this leads us to another major misconception. Just as physical marriage was not created by God, divorce follows as well.

When two souls choose to come together, it is primarily to work out individual soul issues, pay off karmic debt or merely to help one or more souls to grow and mature in their development.

It two souls separate; it is due to two primary reasons. First, it may be due to completion of whatever mission they agreed to finish. Or two, for some reason, they have decided that finished or not; they no longer wish to continue their work together. In this instance, they merely return for another incarnation to complete the unfinished soul lesson. It is always a choice through one's free will.

Marriage and divorce themselves have absolutely nothing to do with the path of a soul. They may need to marry due to constraints within the physical world, but that is all. The stigma that is attached to both marriage and divorce is purely man made. Won't millions of souls be in for a surprise when this is realized in the world of Spirit?

We shall conclude our discussion for now.

Be at peace.

Council of Elders

These messages are for all souls that are searching for truth within the self. The purpose is to learn about the inner workings of the universe. Though one may feel it is minute in its form of knowledge, over the learning period it will be considerable knowledge.

The inner soul exists as three dimensional. This is the basis of all form from plant, mineral, up to physical manifestation of the human body. We will go into more detail on this later. For now, this sentence must generate within you and this energy be allowed to resonate on all levels.

For the most part, a young soul begins its journey free of outside influences. Over time, many influences, both outside and inside, occur through what has been pre-programmed to happen.

You are correct that everything is predestined. This concept is difficult for many souls to comprehend. Any soul in distress wants to believe that whatever happens, for them, they have no responsibility. They believe it comes from outside them, not from within. Everything comes from within. It may come from different levels, but it all comes from within.

One can either see they are responsible, or they can choose to see themselves as a victim. Either way, they must come eventually to realize their responsibility within themselves.

For example, a distressful situation occurs. A soul reacts to it instead of flowing with it. Then through meditation, sleep state, dreams, guidance, or deep thinking; they realize a different way of response.

In changing the vibration of thought, they begin to change the vibration of the outcome. How often has something happened where your thoughts in the moment turned it into a mountain when it was simply a molehill?

Remember, most of all, it's all about the energy. Energy can only be transformed. Reflect on times where you were strong in your feeling or decision. Then, when you took it to a higher level of thought, the energy transformed into something completely different.

For now, we have begun to give you enough for contemplation. We shall conclude for now and bless you.

Enoch and the Council of 7

Good evening. Today, we wish to discuss another avenue for soul development. Each soul chooses the means by which to learn various virtues. They may choose one or more virtues in an incarnation. Eventually, each virtue must be mastered in order to succeed from the wheel of reincarnation.

Along with this, a soul may aid another soul by playing a role to help them master their virtues. Notice how a volatile spark of energy is enough to bring the emotion of a virtue to the surface. Remember, once again, it is merely energy and this energy can be transformed.

The true soul, in its understanding, must realize the role of emotions taking place. Emotions are the catalyst for many areas. When a soul's emotions erupt to the surface, they are unable, in that moment, to see through the illusion or to identify the role that is being played.

Think of the times when you take a breath and step back from certain situations. What happens when you do? Is the energy of your thoughts transformed? What happens to the emotions?

We speak often of the center or core of your being. If you truly operate from your center in a state of peace- then nothing can disrupt you. No person or situation will cause any disturbance. Yet, if you operate outside of this center; then havoc can rule.

Ponder these avenues and you will find a great deal of substance. Each moment is an opportunity for growth. Seize it and learn.

Blessings,

Council of 7

Good evening. We wish to once again discuss aspects of soul development. One aspect each soul must master is the virtue of patience. As part of the human experience, one discovers individual patience and the degree to which they have mastered it. Over time, patience can become a major factor in one's own surroundings.

Humans, over time, often become less patient and less tolerant of themselves and others around them. The more impatient they become, the more options of the lesson are experienced. You can observe the impatience of those around you in various degrees. Look at the amount of road rage that is experienced today. Look at the people impatient when they merely are waiting in a line.

Humans tend to want things to happen in their own time and when it doesn't, their impatience reaches a peak. Once again it goes back to one's core center. When a soul operates from their center of peace, no person or experience can upset that calm, and therefore impatience does not become an issue. No matter what is going on around them, they exude the energy of patience.

Think about experiences of being in line where you can visually see people become impatient to varying degrees. The more impatient they become, the more upset and possibly vocal they become. Yet, one person in that experience remains calm as if they have all the time in the world.

Many times, that one person can affect others in a positive way as opposed to the one using impatience to cause disruption.

Now, within each soul exists a blueprint of energy for the individual. There is also a universal energy blueprint, which incorporates all individual soul blueprints. Along with that, is an imprint of energy for all the experiences one has with others, imprinted within their individual pattern. Let us try to put this in perspective to better aid you in understanding.

1) Each soul has an individual blueprint.

2) All experiences with others have an imprint placed within the individual's blueprint.

3) Both the individual blueprint and the imprint of all experiences are layered into and part of the universal blueprint.

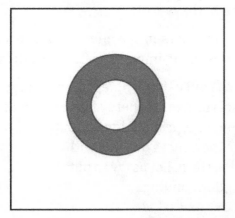

Each is affected by the energy of their own blueprint and the imprint of others. The energy is all connected. Think about being very calm and walking into an area of a group of people who are all in a hurry to be someplace. They can't move fast enough because there are too many people. Immediately, the mood becomes impatient and everyone becomes caught up in it, which escalates the situation. The one who entered in a state of calm knows they must get out of there in order to remain calm or get back to that calm.

Whenever a soul's state of being is disrupted; they must ask themselves a number of questions:

1) Why am I beginning to feel a sense of disruption or impatience?
2) Is this coming from within me or is it part of the imprint of someone around me?
3) To return to one's center, one must take several deep breaths, breathing in peace and calm and exhaling frustration and disruption.

Remember, energy is energy. It can never be destroyed, merely transformed.

One of the greatest lessons in life is that realization and learning how to deal with the energy in and around you.

Universal Law will guide the energy to offer you the greatest state of being. However, one must operate within Universal Law to operate the best possible way from one's own center of being.

This concludes our discussion for this evening.

Blessings,

Council of 12

CHAPTER 11

Good evening and thank you. We wish to speak of soul diversity and the true nature of the soul.

The true nature of the soul evolves from its own dimension. This is the purest of all dimensions. It is where the spark ignites and is born. It is purity in its finest form. Here is where the highest realms exist.

From there, a soul continues slowly through the other dimensions and begins incarnations. Thus, begins the life of the soul, one lifetime and dimension at a time.

This entire package as it may be, goes beyond being overwhelming to the individual. It is within these life incarnations and dimensions that growth and development take place. Here is where behaviors and patterns begin.

As a soul continues to exist simultaneously in other dimensions, so does their development. A soul may be working on or mastering one pattern or behavior on one dimension while working on the exact opposite behavior or pattern in another dimension. Yet, we are connected within the individual soul collectively on all dimensions.

One may often speak of layers and this could not have more truth. It may be one layer on one dimension, and four or five other layers in other dimensions.

The final result is the same. For a soul to succeed from reincarnation, all the layers must be peeled to the core, only to resurface whole and complete. Thus, truth and purity are restored.

Please ponder this teaching. There is a great deal which dwells within it.

Council of 12

Good evening. Tonight, we shall discuss the roll of intuition and soul development. When a soul incarnated in the past, the depth of the veil covering them was strong. Generally, it took a major life changing event for the veil to crack, so to speak, and light energy from the other realms to flow though. As a result, sometimes an awakening began and sometimes it did not happen.

A soul would make the choice whether change occurred or not. For some, it was immediate, for others, denial was stronger, and their lives continued as before until another programmed event within them appeared. That point was another opportunity presenting itself.

As time progressed, after many lifetimes, the souls reincarnating have a thinner veil and more awareness as a whole.

Whenever a soul begins to awaken, it affects every soul. Some new souls entering now have awareness and recall at an incredibly young age.

One avenue which greatly fosters awareness is intuition. A soul, through their energy field, feels their intuition or gut instinct as you may call it. The more they use and follow that intuition, the greater impact it has on day to day life. The more denial of the intuition, the more closed off that intuitive energy becomes.

A soul may choose a different route or travel without understanding why; yet they know they had to go that way. Later, they find the previous choice or road was shut down due to an accident or construction.

Each time a soul chooses to follow their intuition, it is like climbing a mini ladder one step at a time.

Be aware of your intuitive choices and let them flow through you and one's life will flow much smoother.

This concludes our lesson for tonight.

Blessings,

Council of 12

Good evening. Tonight's discussion will be on integration of personality aspects and the role dreams play in development.

Many avenues are used in soul development, one of which is dreams. It is a strong role in which we can gain immediate access on many levels to provide knowledge and wisdom.

Be clear on this: **All** dreams are orchestrated for soul development. Different experiences a soul has during the day are often utilized. This facilitates the dream planning due to the imprint of the experience already being present.

We need only to touch into the energy of that imprint to redistribute the energy, for it to be present in the dream.

Dreams vary in how they are presented. They may be long or short, simple, or complex. It simply depends on what a soul needs for growth in that period of existence.

If a strong presence is needed, a soul will repeat the same dream. It may happen to repeat in the same night; it may happen for several days and then a nightmare is experienced, or it may happen over many days or weeks. What matters is the amount of attention given to it.

If a soul discounts the dream, you can be sure another event with the same learning experience will occur. Repeated dreams and nightmares are given as attention seeking means to preempt that same experience. If offers the soul another option of choice.

A soul who states, "I never remember my dreams", or "I don't dream", is merely one whose darkness surrounds them in a thickness, and by choice they are not interested in looking beyond the darkness.

We still attempt to reach all souls, knowing it is merely one avenue. Sometimes along the way an event, experience, or choice will happen to open the door to further growth.

More will be discussed at a later time. This concludes tonight's discussion.

Council of 24

Greetings from the Divine Feminine. There are many who wish to enter your energy to share in knowledge and wisdom.

As a soul matures in development, it is the Divine Feminine which plays a major role. It is this aspect of soul which guards and rules other aspects. Each segment of this aspect, and there are thirty-three, can be reached in various realms. This soul attribute and its aspects create a macrocosm in the energy of the soul.

It is vital for the basic masculine and feminine energies to be mastered. This must include the integration of soul fragments. Until this integration takes place, the merging and balance of the masculine and feminine cannot be accomplished.

This would be like trying to merge two energies into one when they had holes and gaps. It would not work. The soul fragments must be healed and integrated before true balance and merging can take place.

Let your soul realize what has been spoken here for now. This shall suffice.

Blessings,

Divine Feminine

CHAPTER 12

Good evening. Tonight, we would like to speak about the transference of energy.

Every soul throughout one's day, transfers energy to everything and everyone around them. A simple hello said to another is a transfer of energy.

Whether balanced or imbalanced energy, such as an argument, it is still a transfer of energy. When a soul feels good and expresses a conversation with another soul, there is a transfer of energy which can lift up another soul.

The other end of the spectrum happens when another soul discharges their own imbalanced energy. It is still energy put out into the universe.

We hear you use the phrase, "it doesn't have anything to do with you." While this is true, the energy put out there is still seeking a target so to speak through Universal Law of Attraction.

If a soul operates from their center of peace and calm, then the energy merely searches for another like target, and they will not be affected. Yet, until the soul is centered in peace, they often become affected by the energy around them.

Think about your daily experiences, where and how you transfer energy. If you feel good and are happy, you smile at people, lifting their spirits as well as your own.

Now, think of an event that happens where you become frustrated or upset with something someone else did or said. What happens? Does it affect you, your day and interaction with others, or do you operate from your center of calm without the energy affecting you?

Using your energy is a choice. We are only influenced by another's energy when we allow it. One must have balance within their own energy to override the effect of another's energy.

Look at the events of your day and how the transference of energy affects you. As you well know, the Law of Karma-whether in grand or minute scale-will be experienced.

Each individual soul can choose whether to allow another's energy to affect or upset their own balance or not.

Think of when you feel good, are having a good day, until you encounter someone experiencing just the opposite. Do you allow it to affect you? Do you try to lift that soul and transform that energy? Or does it become part of your energy through transference, which is then continued through your day.

Every day a soul can choose which energy they wish to express and transfer-energy for the good of all, energy from the opposite end of the spectrum, or anything in between.

We use this lesson and discussion so one may reflect on their own energy and that which they transfer to others.

Choose wisely always for its impact is one drop of water in the vastness of the ocean that has a ripple effect throughout the universe.

Good evening and blessings to you.

Council of 12

Good evening. Tonight, we shall speak of the moment of death. Prior to this point, a soul's state of being varies from total lucidity to a complete state of coma, or anything in between. It depends on what the soul has experienced whether due to a long illness or a quick event such as an accident.

For the purpose of this transcription, we shall not include suicides.

Even those in various states of sleep or coma, often show signs of rallying just prior to death. This often gives loved ones a sense of peace or comfort and the opportunity to say goodbye.

The moment of death is merely a process of going from one dimension and the physical body, to leaving the density behind and acquiring the spirit body, which was merely encapsulated within the physical body. In order for others to understand, it is much like a body of live energy being inside the hard shell of the physical body. At the moment of death, as the physical body, or shell, begins to age and break down, the shell cracks open, disintegrates, and allows the energy body to emerge and separate from the physical body.

Once this energy or spirit body separates, the soul is often confused as to what has happened. Prior to this, guides and angels have been working with the soul in preparation for this transition. Still, this beginning period takes a great deal of understanding for the soul. It is a period of acclimation to learn not only how things work, but also a great deal of time is spent discarding the traits and beliefs taught and learned while on earth.

Until this all has been accepted and absorbed, the soul is not ready for more development. In general, some souls take longer than others. It depends on the depth of their belief and whether it was truth, or merely religious instruction or doctrine. No one is forced to accept anything until each soul is ready.

Prior to this point, many are sent to healing hospitals where the energy of the soul can be rejuvenated until they are pure in form.

This shall conclude our discussion for this evening. We bid you many blessings.

Council of 12

Good evening. Let us begin. The goal of our council is to educate mankind so that the individual vibration, the collective vibration and the planetary vibration can be raised.

Through each soul development there is a ripple effect on everything both positive or balanced, and negative or imbalanced.

We seek to bring balance in all things so that our worlds may exist in harmony. This is the preservation of all.

Peace begins within the individual soul. It is the drop of light that gives birth to peace within all.

You were both chosen to be part of this mission, one after the other, one beside the other, yet always together, firmly embedded within each other and the ALL.

Your service, no matter how large or small does not go unnoticed. Each soul serves in their own way. Some are guided through knowledge and intuition; others are guided through misinformation and knowledge.

You are both guided from the Councils, the higher echelons from which all comes. Never doubt your mission. Never doubt your service.

We shall always provide your direction, your path, your journey.

Be still and know your Gods and know we are here always.

God's blessings upon you.

Council of 24

Good evening. Tonight, we shall begin to explore new topics of development. Some may have been touched on previously. However, as we continue to expand the topics, new avenues are activated within the individual soul.

Soul energy begins with the essence of the soul being pristine in nature. As a soul enters an incarnation, the purity of essence continues. Then life begins to happen. As they grow and develop, the events and experiences impact the soul energy field.

If an experience is felt to be traumatic for the individual soul, the soul energy field may deem the experience as threatening. When this happens, a piece of the soul may fragment. It may disappear into a body part to hide, or it may move to a place outward in the aura. These are just a few scenarios. This fragmented part will do what is necessary for it to feel a sense of safety and security.

Those experiences, whether real or imagined are seen through and perceived at the age of the soul during the event. Although the human being continues to age, grow, and develop, the soul fragment is trapped in the same age as when the event occurs.

When these fragments split, it affects many areas. Often the void is felt through perception and emotions. They may feel "empty" or "not all there". It may involve another individual in which they have given up their power to another soul.

The fragment may be experienced in the current life, or it can be the result of a past life. For healing and integration to take place, the cord must be traced back to the core event.

For each incarnation, the goal for every soul is to operate with complete wholeness of the energy field. Wholeness within exudes the best possible means for greatest soul growth.

Development comes from the knowledge, wisdom and understanding that is derived from soul retrieval and bringing them home.

Once a fragment is experienced, it often becomes easier for a subsequent event. It may even be a shocking event that was a happy occasion. It is the shock which can causes a piece of soul energy to split. The soul energy dwells within total peace and tranquility. Therefore, you can understand why anything beyond the balance of peace and tranquility can cause disruption, and subsequently separation or fragmentation.

This concludes tonight's discussion.

Blessings,

Council of 24

Today is the beginning of universal solidarity. The alignment of the earth's sky will impact most of the souls there. Only those born from the new generation will remain either unaffected or mildly affected.

What you feel around you is a state of chaos and confusion. This alignment dispels unbalanced energy. The chaos will ease over the next three to four days and pretty much be settled within a week's time.

It is important for both of you to stay centered and to meditate. There we can ease the effects of this energy.

There are also a variety of events taking place in the world which also impacts the cosmos. Egypt and global warming have the greatest impact right now. The wars going on had the most affect when they started. The longer they persist, the less effect they have. It is because the longer it occurs, the milder the impact. When a new uprising occurs, there is the greatest immediate impact. That is the present state of Egypt.

Once again it is part of Divine Law and each part of what takes place has its own purpose. It is about the growth of the soul and what is learned from their experiences.

For now, this information will suffice. We will meet again soon.

Council of 7

We would like to talk to you about discovery. Discovery plays an important role throughout a soul's journey. Along with discovery comes interpretation and perception. They each may or may not include illusion. As we grow in understanding, we begin to discover things about ourselves, our truth and our perception.

What we see about ourselves may seem totally inaccurate through another's eyes. Who is correct? It depends on their amount of soul growth. If we see through the personality, it is a totally different perception. If we see through our higher self, then many distortions will be eliminated. We must also see through the eyes of honesty.

Other times, seeing truth may then involve the ego. The ego will berate, chastise or belittle, but that is not truth.

We forget that perfection exists in us all. We are merely playing the role at hand. Keep that in mind. All is being played out just as it should be. It is learning about ourselves and others through experience.

Many souls have climbed into the depts of darkness and climbed back out. What the soul designed has been more than accomplished. Throughout one's life, treat others in the best possible way with kindness and compassion.

The journey involves your own fears, insecurities, envy, and jealousy. These are the hurdles.

It matters not what you see, only what is experienced. Throughout your journey, the perception changes and often your own interpretation. That is growth. As you remove expectations, you foster more learning.

From learning comes growth and knowledge; this leads to truth and wisdom.

Picture a flower seed planted in soil. It needs sun, water, and air to grow. These are constant for it to survive into a healthy plant. Too much sun and it may wither and die. Too much water and it will drown. It is all about the balance of needed elements.

The path is one of constant choices. Some may seem better than others, but one learns from them all. Sometimes, one must repeat a poor choice over and over before they understand and can change that choice. Often it is a revelation.

There are many around all souls to aid where necessary. They help you as well as helping themselves. Many lessons can be worked out through another soul with permission.

The realm of understanding goes far beyond the earth plane. That is merely a drop in the bucket. Certain levels must be obtained before other worlds may be experienced. This is necessary due to the level of advancement of the world.

Otherwise, it would be like an ancient vehicle in a world where everything is through thought. The vehicle is trying to start using the old way of doing things without any knowledge or understanding of thought.

Blessings,

Council of 24

This brings forth another opportunity for understanding. Each soul develops in its own time and with a great deal of help from other souls.

When a soul has completed its journey for an incarnation, it may exit in various points from the physical body.

Once it is separated, it will go to one of many different levels of existence. Much goes into deciding which level a soul has obtained. A great deal depends not only on the growth that has been reached, but also the corresponding beliefs that exist within that growth.

Each soul must advance in such a way as to open themselves to new beliefs and allow themselves to release old patterns of belief. Often, this can be difficult for a soul to accomplish. It a soul is deeply embedded within a certain belief system; it becomes difficult for them to even acknowledge another opportunity.

The cell structure is such that it is like a closed door. They believe they are right in their beliefs and their way is the only way. Therefore, they go to a level of where that same belief system exists. Only through time will a soul begin to question and even then, as you say, "it may take eons of time".

Picture a closed door. Outside this door are many new opportunities for a soul. If the door is closed, no advancement can occur. Only when one seeks to question, or to see the guidance available, can change begin to happen. Then the door may be open just a crack, but it is a beginning. From here many opportunities are available.

It is an entirely different experience for a soul who constantly questions and is open to new advancement of beliefs within an incarnation. We shall further this discussion at another time. Enough for today. We bid you well.

Council of ALL

CHAPTER 13

Blessings of the Universe be upon you. I come to you from the Angelic Realm. I am known here as Angel 32615. My numbers are significant only here in our world. I serve in one of two capacities. One, you refer to as the Pink Lady. The other for your purposes shall be known as one of the Blue Ladies.

As a soul readies itself to incarnate, they are assigned an angel. You refer to them as a guardian angel. Their role is to stay with the individual soul throughout all their incarnations. They record all that happens, all that is experienced and the results.

These angels give aid, comfort and protection when needed and asked for by the soul.

An angel, or guide may enter only so far until the soul asks for help through thought and prayer. They only guide, never telling a soul what to do-merely offering suggestions from which the soul may make a choice.

Yet, they may not interfere in karmic law. For example: A soul's ego may interfere to the point where they think they have all the answers, do not need anyone's help and don't want any help. In this time, we must merely stand by helplessly watching whatever choice is made. Until they seek wisdom, guidance or help in any form, our hands are tied.

When a new soul enters a realm, the blue lady stands with them for all time and incarnations. When it comes time for a soul to return home, a pink lady appears as an escort. In this capacity we educate, guide and work with the soul long before their exit process begins.

It is the communication through the higher self where much of this process takes place. Eventually, when attained, it filters down to the physical consciousness. This does not always happen before leaving the physical body.

It is much easier when it does. Their transition is smoother, their re-orientation into spirit world is much easier.

Yet, there are instances where a soul, either through stubborn religious beliefs or other means, is so focused on what is ingrained in them, that they refuse to believe any other information. When this happens, they eventually will leave but their re-entry here is much more difficult and takes longer.

Eventually, they come around to see truth and we patiently wait until they do. It is our job to be of service in all capacities.

This concludes our teaching for now. We shall come again another time.

Angel Blessings,

32615

Today we wish to begin discussing the aspects of Universal Law. For everything to flow correctly, there had to be laws that were imposed throughout the universe. These laws reflect all planes of existence and all levels.

Within these laws flow time and space. This occurs on the earth plane where the measure comes through linear time. Linear time does not exist elsewhere. Its purpose was to provide a measurement that worked within the density of the energy on the earth plane, and one that could be understood by the masses.

Within the universe there is no time and space. For many, this understanding seems illogical. They can't comprehend because they think inside the box.

Scientists have helped to provide knowledge which supports Universal Law. Yet, for the masses, it still is confusing. The average person may not understand quantum physics, yet it provides a link to all universal law.

Everything in the universe, all levels and all worlds are happening together in each moment. Yet, the difficulty in comprehending this aspect takes a long time to overcome. For some souls, an experience may occur that removes them from linear time and space, while providing the opportunity to see and experience beyond what they know. This seed will open the door to seeking a part of the bigger picture.

For some souls, the spiritual truth they seek helps aid the knowledge of Universal Law. Yet, other souls may never see or understand beyond the density within the incarnation. Once transition occurs, they are provided the experience of nonlinear time and space. Eventually, as a soul progresses through the wheel of incarnations, they come to face the aspect of nonlinear time. This is one of the most important aspects. It is much like crossing a large bridge from one side to the other. It begins to bridge the gap between the earth plane and other worlds.

Still, even though a soul may be aware of this aspect, they don't necessarily put it to use. They get caught up within the energy of the earth plane and forget the role this aspect provides.

This has provided enough knowledge for the moment. Integrate the energy of this lesson and allow it to become wisdom.

Be at peace,

Council of 24

Good day and we thank you for this time. We continue providing the necessary information.

Today, we will discuss methods of advancement within one's journey. There are several modes of advancement available to all.

One, which we shall label timetable advancement, occurs in the following way. This happens prior to an incarnation and with guidance available. A soul will decide to implement certain events or experiences at a designated period of time to present opportunities for growth and advancement. These would be known on a subconscious and soul level. When they present themselves, it is through an individual choice that one advances.

Things may occur in your plane in the following way. Two souls appear on earth. One soul chooses to go through life seeking any and all help available throughout the life journey. A second soul chooses to go through life completely on his own merit. He chooses not to seek any help and even refuses all help that is offered.

A third venue is a combination of the two means and may be known as time relegated distribution. A soul chooses a particular event or experience and places it within a time period. Along with the event, a period of time exists where the soul chooses self-discovery and awareness of the lesson.

However, if the soul has no self-discovery within the designated time frame, then immediate help and guidance are presented so nothing is lost. This growth is often like a rung on a ladder and can make a huge difference as far as maturity.

Each of these is available to all souls. The greater a soul advances, often the choice of more difficult advancement will occur. Some souls choose to do things the hard way, while another may choose the way providing the most aid available. It is all about growth and choices.

More will be discussed later. This concludes our lesson for now.

Blessings,

Council of 24

Good morning. Our topic deals with acknowledgement and reso-lution. Each moment or period in a soul's life will consist of both these components. It becomes a choice to see them or a choice to instead live in denial. It is through our experiences that acknowl-edgement tries to speak. When we can acknowledge what is occurring, there will be truth behind it. When we deny the acknowledgement, we deny the truth.

Each life involves finding truth within our perception. Sometimes we find it ourselves, but often we discover it through another soul. It matters not how it occurs, but only that we see it.

Each truth will bring a greater understanding. Acknowledging our own truth helps to allow the veil between the worlds to begin to dissipate. Only then will clarity and understanding seep into be-ing.

It also involves trust and intuition. Our intuition comes from our higher self. We can either accept or ignore the feelings of intuition that come from inside.

As we acknowledge that intuition, we expand our awareness and begin resolution on a soul level. Often it takes many experiences where we ignore our intuition and only in hindsight can we rec-ognize the truth of a situation. Still, this is a learning experience.

Once we can acknowledge our intuition, we begin to realize its power. If we allow it, our intuition proves a great aid to finding and acknowledging our truth.

Ponder these thoughts and we shall speak later.

Many blessings from us all,

Council of 18

Good evening. Tonight, we shall discuss the nature of soul union. When two souls come together it is for many reasons.

For some, there are one or more contracts that are agreed upon before one's incarnation. The souls have agreed to come together to aid one another in soul development, both individually and collectively.

When the agreement has been accomplished, the soul may choose to separate. This can happen through separation, divorce, illness, or death. Once the agreed upon actions and growth have occurred, the soul is free to move on.

Yet, some souls may decide to stay in their present surroundings and conditions. Other souls choose to come in to aid humanity, in any way, shape or form. These souls will have one experience after another that will help to raise the collective vibration of energy. Often, they are old souls that have experienced a multitude of events designed purely to help the Natural Law of Balance between dark and light energy.

This merely offers a few scenarios of soul union and explanations. For each soul, the dynamics differs. Some of the greatest growth and development occurs during their time with other contracted souls. For others, it does not occur until after one soul has moved on.

Reflection and hindsight offer great aid in opening one's eyes and perceptions.

There is great food for thought within these words. Ponder them.

Namaste,

Council of 24

CHAPTER 14

Good evening. Tonight, we shall discuss the energy disposition of soul fields. As a soul begins the exit process, their energy field remains intact, yet it is two different areas. There is the soul field energy body and the soul field of the physical body.

At the moment of death, the energy of the soul field is released from the physical body. Although the two bodies have been meshed as one, they now begin their separation.

The energy of the soul field body moves on while the energy body of the physical body begins to dissipate. Where the energy soul field gave life to the physical energy field, that no longer occurs.

There are various levels of energies within both the soul field body and the physical field body. The energies that exist on a higher vibration are absorbed into the soul field body while all other energies begin to dissipate.

As the soul field body begins to move on through the process, a purification begins. Depending on the soul's level of advancement, this process may be long or short in duration. For a novice, it may take a great deal of time whereas an old soul returning home allows the process to occur much more rapidly.

There is a great deal of information to digest here. This concludes our discussion.

Blessings,

Council of 24

Good evening. Tonight, we shall discuss soul anatomy. Soul anatomy is comprised of all the elements within one's being. The soul encompasses everything about the individual as well as collective consciousness.

There are many who would disagree with that statement. They seek to restrict the meaning of one soul to the individual being. Yet, we speak in terms of energy. It would be like saying a drop of the ocean is just one drop, rather than the drop being part of the entire ocean. The drop alone is a drop of water. Yet, when placed within the body of water which is the ocean, it merges with and becomes a part of the larger whole. It is individual, and it is collective.

Such is the same with the soul. Everything about a soul exists within them and yet through the collective consciousness, everything exists within them about all souls.

This presents new perspective about the existence of all things.

May you ponder the wisdom of these words.

Blessings,

Council of 24

Good day to you. Today we wish to continue our discussion. The manner of segments is quite important. Within the segments are twenty-seven levels. These consist of all things necessary for completeness of an incarnation.

Some levels have to do with particulars that involve the personality and the ego. Others involve recognition of soul aspects. Each is necessary for completeness. All is accomplished through experience.

Most often the experience takes place with the aid of others. It merely depends on the role being played.

Peace must be made with each element within each segment. When peace occurs, then thoughts of the experience are no longer revisited. When a soul continuously revisits the past, it causes the energy of the event or experience to be stirred. It gives it new life so to speak. The more thought that is generated, the more life given to it. That is why it is so important to release the past, not dwell on it. It is usually our emotions that cause us to revisit the past.

One must remember we are here to learn. That is the purpose. We have not done anything wrong. One choice may seem better than another, but we learn from them all. When we constantly revisit the past, it merely causes the lesson to be revisited over and over again.

One must choose, recognize, acknowledge and release (CRAR). This is the ticket to freedom. Make the best choice you can at that moment. Recognize what is experienced within that choice. Acknowledge what has been learned and seen. Then release the experience; let go. In this way a great deal is accomplished.

This concludes our time for today.

Blessings,

Council of 24

Hello. Once again, we wish to speak of a few things. We enter your realm whenever the opportunity presents itself. Still, we respect your free will as well.

Might we also state that our mission is purely brought forth to change the vibration of the entire mass consciousness. For eons of time, the battle has existed between the light and the dark. It has always been there, while sometimes more obvious than others.

When the Harmonic conversion took place, it brought forth new opportunities in which the energy pattern of the grid could be elevated in a way that would greatly benefit all. Each time we have an opportunity such as this, we fully utilize it.

There are many changes which occur as a result. Some that are what you call destructive, are merely a complete cleansing which occurs through the means of Natural Law. By this, we speak of floods, fires, earthquakes, etc. This is mother nature's way of the transformation of energy when needed. Although it is viewed as purely destructive in nature; it is transformative.

Think not of only the act itself, but of what is transformed because of the act. Whether a soul is involved in the actual act or not, they are still affected on many levels.

How many times have you heard an individual who has experienced what is seen as devasting, say it was the best thing that could have happened to them?

This is the soul speaking of a transformation. These are all awakening events for the soul.

There has been misrepresentation that has fostered for eons of time. The mission is to dispel much of that information. We will use whatever means possible to provide the most widespread attention we can deliver. We ask only for you to be open to our call.

This shall suffice for this moment in time.

Council of ALL

Good day to you. This teaching is about the Law of Balance. For complete balance to occur within the individual soul, there must be balance on all levels: physical, emotional, mental, and spiritual. You can see, therefore the great degree of imbalance that exists. While one area may be in balance, complete balance does not exist.

The key to keeping balance is through monitoring the level of one's own energy. The higher the energy vibration, the easier balance can result. This must coincide, however, with the individual's healing work on themselves. Should there only be meditation without individual soul work, the higher vibration cannot be sustained and therefore complete balance will not occur. It is in doing the individual work that speeds the process of balance.

Many choose to stay in a state of attachment thinking that in helping and serving others, they are helping themselves. The reality, it is only in helping themselves that they can help others. Detachment is key.

When one seeks balance, it is balance of self, first. Again, this has a ripple effect by raising all energy around them. They help the "whole" by helping themselves.

As the numbers are perfected by the individual soul, the energy of the matrix is elevated. All is within the Divine, remember that. The darkness, destruction, war, etc...and the light, beauty and love energy are all part of the vibration. They are all One, each vibration is part of the whole, part of the Divine Plan. Ponder these thoughts today.

Blessings,

Council of 24

Each aspect of a soul must be integrated. Often, this is the same as what you call soul fragments.

There are times when spiritual advisors will generate energy from that divided aspect. They will delve into the cellular memory in order to bring the incident to the surface. This incident may have been buried for lifetimes.

In doing this, it sometimes can help bring that energy into conscious awareness. It may take numerous attempts for this to occur. The incident or experience can be brought through dream state, or simply as a flash of memory in the waking state.

This process can bring a re-entry into the whole, what is considered a fragment. Fragments may also be integrated while in spirit world, but it is more complex to do so and will take a much greater period of time. This once again is food for thought.

Council of 7

Good evening. Tonight, we wish to speak about soul integration. When a soul chooses to incarnate, they choose what developmental aspects they desire to master. This can occur over many lifetimes.

Depending on their awareness, they discover what work is needed and in what area of their soul development. For example, one soul may have the same experience over and over, without ever questioning or searching for why it keeps on happening. Therefore, they disregard any type of response that would change the energy of the outcome.

Another soul, having these same experiences, questions why they keep on happening and searches for what is needed to change the dynamics and the resulting outcome.

When discovery occurs, the integration begins. For a soul to integrate aspects, they must first have mastered them. There are various degrees of the age of aspects, must like soul fragments.

Aspects, or parts of the soul, split off because of their experiences, mostly through fear. It is much like a child who has a fearful experience and runs away to hide. For others, it is a matter of shutting parts of themselves off as a means of protection.

Whenever this happens, it is the result of a prior experience rearing its head, usually from fear.

Resolution must occur for each soul. For some, it can go back to many previous lifetimes; for others, it can be the current lifetime or even yesterday. It must be resolved back to the core or the origin, for integration to occur.

Once the issues of the aspects are mastered, the integration begins to take place. It is an automatic occurrence through Universal Law.

Some souls never realize it happens, while others may see or feel the shift in their energy. The fear begins to recede until its eventually non-existent.

The goal of every soul is full integration of all aspects in order to succeed from the wheel of reincarnation.

This concludes our discussion for now.

Blessings,

Council of 12

CHAPTER 15

Today, we would like to give more understanding to healing of an aspect. Each aspect is a living breathing part. It has its own consciousness. When an aspect divides, it is as if an atom or cell has split off from the whole. It is separate and on its own, yet still connected to the whole all at the same time.

What can happen is that it takes on its own life, own energy. It is influenced by its own thought and those around it. So, therefore the energy increases. What may have started as a small separation, has now ballooned in size. Each experience can help or hinder, depending on the incident.

The longer the separation exists, often the healing is more difficult. This is one reason why it is so important to search for and integrate all parts of self.

They more that are integrated, the more unity and wholeness occurs. It is about bringing this vital energy back into the fold.

Blessings,

Council of 7

Today's lesson will be about self-realization and discovery. There are many avenues to reach this goal. The goal consists of the subject being about themselves as well as others. Often our own self-discovery or realization comes through the avenue of others.

We can often become aware of things because we may see or experience it through other people. Often, they themselves, are unaware of what is transpiring; yet to us, it may stick out like a sore thumb. We may marvel at the fact that they have no idea it is occurring. This may happen because truly we are the ones who need to see it through their experience, or they may just not be ready for it to be brought into their consciousness awareness.

There is much value either way it happens. For the one who becomes aware or realizes the experience, it appears consciously. For the individual on the other end, it still becomes a part of their unconscious awareness.

We are here on the earth plane for many reasons. Sometimes, a soul may spend an entire lifetime trying to gain conscious self-realization. Perhaps, in their last lifetime, they had the experience but did not have the conscious understanding of the event or situation. Therefore, in this lifetime, they entered into the same events or experiences in order for true conscious discovery to occur.

Just as things must occur "as above, so below", our discovery must involve bringing the light of the conscious awareness into the dark of the unconsciousness. Just think about a time, event, or experience where you suddenly had the realization of truth. It may be something that happened a thousand times, yet in this one thousand and one time, suddenly, like a light bulb going off, you finally had the self-realization that you needed in this lesson.

People get hung up on why the same situations or experiences keep happening to them. It is *ONLY* because they need to discover what it is that they seek to learn for their soul development. Two souls may be intertwined merely for the purpose of helping each other through their individual lessons and challenges of a certain lifetime.

Each role, each person, each experience that is going on in a soul's life, all has purpose. It is up to the individual soul to discover what that purpose may be.

Also, let us remind you that all must be in accordance with Universal Law. Each experience and lesson must be part of a Universal Law. That is why we seek to educate souls in the knowledge of this law. When they can understand the laws, they can begin to understand the workings of the universe.

Once that happens, they can truly begin to live the life they were meant to live. No more self-pity, no more being the victim, no more being the martyr. They begin to understand the value of the lessons. They can them reap the benefits of the education. From there the soul growth occurs often for them and may even involve others as well.

Living through Universal Laws is far greater and far more pleasant than going against them. When an individual has struggle in life; it may be that they are going against the Universal Laws instead of living within the laws.

Just think about the laws of earth, legal laws. What happens when someone lives within the law? Life may be smooth. Then think of someone who refuses to live within those laws and purposely goes against them. They end up arrested, in jail or spending time in prison. That prison was self-imposed!

So, when one can focus on living within the laws of the universe, they find that the life and even their lessons will flow much smoother.

Reflect on this teaching and live each day to the fullest extent.

Many blessings upon you,

Council of Twelve

CHAPTER 16

Good day to you. Today we wish to speak about soul trials. There are three trials that exist within a soul's journey. Two of them occur within a certain period during the journey. It may be different for each soul. These will often occur during a major event in the soul's life. It is the experience that creates the trial.

It is set up to discover what the soul has attained in knowledge and understanding thus far. It is evaluated through their strengths and weaknesses. It also shows what is necessary in order to further help the soul in their journey.

Their attitude will play a part. Are they open to receive help, or have they closed the door and given up? Once again it is a choice.

Before a soul's final exit, the trial comes in a different circumstance. They will be asked questions and the answers will be examined. It is necessary before one can be processed through their exit point. Much of the processing is done during the dream state. This helps to explain the depth of their state of sleep. This is by design.

For each soul to have complete recall would be at a disadvantage in their conscious world. Also, the energy within the work being done would be too elevated within the earth plane.

Picture a world of complete harmony. Then try to bring that into an imbalanced world with tremendous magnetic fields. This gives an inkling of what has transpired within the soul.

We constantly work to shift the energy, to ease one's transition.

Blessings to all,

Council of 18

Thank you for answering. We wish to speak about self-actualization. Within each soul exists cell memory from each lifetime experienced. As a soul recognizes the lessons within a past life, there is a change within the cell structure.

As the memory of the lesson is actualized within the soul, the cell structure is cleansed and purified. When this happens, that fragment of the soul is absorbed back into the whole, thus changing the cell structure. As a result, that lesson is completed, never to be repeated.

Picture a matrix of moving dashes - - - - -, only within the structure are gaps - - - - - - - - - - -which are lessons needed to be fulfilled. As they are fulfilled and actualized within the soul level, the gaps in the matrix are filled.

Each part of every soul must fulfill their own lessons, to complete the matrix. All numbers must be fulfilled in order for a soul to be set free from reincarnation.

As a soul progresses in the knowledge and understanding, this growth can create new hurdles to overcome. These occur within your dense plane. A struggle occurs because the soul no longer feels the comfort they once had there. Their comfort and peace exist on other worlds of like energy. Still, it is necessary for the soul to remain within the earth plane to fulfill their destiny.

This too can be an ongoing struggle. To ease this challenge, one can find solace within nature, the woods, and bodies of water. As you know, the ocean cleanses and refreshes one's soul energy. One must find the means to diminish these struggles.

As one comes closer to their exit point, these struggles begin to diminish. This occurs due to more of the soul energy returning to source.

By the time transition happens, the separation comes quite easily. The more prepared the soul is, the easier the split. This concludes today's lesson.

Be well,

Council of 18

Self-actualization-the process of establishing oneself as a whole person able to develop one's abilities and understand oneself.

Our topic will be more about transference. This occurs on a regular basis.

Transference occurs when energy from one person or place is transferred from that person, place, or object. That energy is not always received by another. It depends on the level of sensitivity of the receiver. If they are completely shut off, it is not received. Both have merit. In a transference of positive or elevated energy, if the receiver is open, it can provide a healing or elevation of their energy.

In an imbalanced form, if it is received, it may produce the opposite effect.

The other instance occurs when the receiver may recognize the imbalance without actually absorbing the energy. Instead, they use it to offer aid to another soul for healing to occur.

The openness of each soul will vary with each circumstance. When one enters a crowd, they are being subjected to many levels of energy. That is why we caution you to recognize your level of openness. It is better to contain your aura and pull it in when you are among the masses of unknown energy.

When you are among those of a more elevated or like energy, then allow your aura to expand. This provides healing for all. It is extremely important to recognize your surroundings on an energetic level.

Please try to put this into action. Often, we are unaware of the energy around us.

Be conscious of what is happening around you. It provides a wealth of learning and understanding. When among the masses, be present in your body. It is far more valuable than you realize.

Blessings,

Council of 18

Chapter 17

We would like to talk about discovery. Discovery plays an important role throughout a soul's journey. Along with discovery comes interpretation and perception. They each may or may not include illusion. As we grow in understanding, we begin to discover things about ourselves, our truth and our perception.

What we see about ourselves may seem totally inaccurate through another's eyes. Who is correct? It depends on their amount of soul growth. If we see through the personality, it is a totally different perception. If we see through our higher self; then many distortions will be eliminated. We must also see through the eyes of honesty.

Other times, seeing truth may then involve the ego. The ego will berate, chastise, or belittle, but that is not truth.

We forget that perfection exists in us all. We are merely playing the role at hand. Keep that in mind. All is being played out just as it should be. We are learning about ourselves and others through experience.

Many souls have climbed into the depths of darkness and climbed back out. What the soul designed has been more than accomplished. Throughout one's life, treat others in the best possible way with kindness and compassion.

The journey involves your own fears, insecurities, envy and jealousy. These are the hurdles.

It matters not what you see, only what is experienced. Throughout your journey, the perception changes and often your own interpretation. That is growth. As you remove expectations, you foster more learning. From learning comes growth and knowledge; this leads to truth and wisdom.

Picture a flower seed planted in soil. It needs sun, water, and air to grow. These are constant for it to survive into a healthy plant. Too much sun and it may wither and die. Too much water and it will drown. It is all about the balance of needed elements.

The path is one of constant choices. Some may seem better than others, but one learns from them all. Sometimes one must repeat a poor choice over and over before they understand and can change that choice. Often it is a revelation.

There are many around all souls to aid where necessary. They help you as well as helping themselves. Many lessons can be worked out through another soul with permission.

The realm of understanding goes far beyond the earth plane. That is merely a drop in the bucket. Certain levels must be obtained before other worlds may be experienced. This is necessary due to the level of advancement of the world. Otherwise, it would be like an ancient vehicle in a world where everything is through thought. The vehicle is trying to start using the old way of doing things, without any knowledge or understanding of thought.

Blessings,

Council of 24

Today we wish to indoctrinate you with more knowledge and understanding of the spirit realm. When one enters this realm at the end of the incarnation, there is a good deal of adjusting that must occur. This is both on an energetic level and with regard to what has transferred on a spiritual and emotional level. In some souls, a good deal is shed at their point of entry, due to their level of advancement, while others come in with clutter from the earth plane.

Souls arriving from other worlds, particularly mental worlds, arrive with a much cleaner and clearer energy field. Those from the earth plane come with more due to the energetic density of the plane.

Those who advance spiritually while on the earth plane are generally working to clear and refine their fields on a regular basis. Some happens even without their knowledge. Time spent in nature or bodies of water, such as the ocean, automatically provide cleansing. Those who spend time in dense magnetic fields, generally have the greatest difficulty.

Here, we have many advancements to remove what is unnecessary. Some souls on re-entry will pick up where they left off, while others can come in with a new level of awareness.

This choice is made before re-entry. Some souls want to be sure of what has been resolved and therefore choose to pick up where they left off. When this occurs, they often will find that their experiences will be expedited. Sometimes, a soul wonders why the particular lesson will reoccur at a much faster rate. This can explain the reason.

Also, as a soul completes the necessary numbers in the matrix, they find the number of lessons and challenges diminish. Life seems to flow smoothly, and they wonder why. As this happens, there is an internal peace that is felt. There is clarity that is seen and felt. It is as if what is learned has been magnified and can be readily seen regarding others.

When this occurs, their intuition of soul becomes acute. They find a quiet within themselves. A soul knows when the job is completed. They see and enjoy what has transpired. Yet still they bask in the opportunity to aid another soul. They look at their world and its surroundings with new eyes. Their enjoyment comes in new ways. They understand what they are leaving.

As they experience these insights, many emotions may surface from strange to wonderful. It cannot be explained, only experienced. It is similar to when you channel an entity, and they enter and experience your physical body. They had forgotten what the physical body felt like. It is quite strange, yet wonderful.

This concludes our lesson for today.

Be at peace,

Council of 24

We wish to continue the lesson. The intention is to offer guidance and understanding in a realm that is unknown to many. We seek to educate the masses and you are one of the vessels we are using.

What is offered to others will have an impact for an exceptionally long time. It will change the vibration of the earth plane. The journey each soul makes is divided into segments. There are 4 segments of each incarnation. Then within each segment are various levels.

A soul will choose how many levels they hope to complete. They may or may not finish them all. It depends on a soul's amount of awareness within each segment.

Some souls may complete each level before moving to the next segment. Others may only complete part of the level, then move on to the next segment. When this occurs, they merely pick them up in the next incarnation.

Some souls refuse to move to another segment until all levels are finished. Their determination supersedes anything else. These are souls who truly seek the greatest amount of wisdom and knowledge within each lifetime.

There comes appoint within each lifetime, where a soul will realize exactly where they are in their level of understanding. For most souls, this is unconscious. For those whose eyes are open through the veil; it is a conscious realization. They may not know to what degree this is accomplished, but through wisdom they begin to see knowledge in action. They truly understand and put knowledge into motion. This is how Buddha was able to complete his incarnations.

For now, this completes our lesson. We will continue this lesson next time. There is a great deal to think about here. Through thought, you allow the energy of wisdom to resonate and grow within your being. Transformation then occurs. We bid you goodbye until next time.

Council of 24

Today we shall discuss the ongoing nature of spirit world. Spirit world is divided into levels. Each level provides the correct energy and atmosphere for each soul.

Where a soul goes after transition, depends not only on their level of development, but also on their belief system and thoughts. What a soul believes is what is initially provided and what is necessary. Only when a soul begins to question and seek more truth, can that change.

In a soul who lives truth, the plane or level of advancement will be realized. There is always aid available and those who arrive still in darkness are constantly offered the necessary aid to be brought into the light. But first, they must see and understand the darkness within themselves. Only when that is realized can change begin to occur.

Souls on various levels can intermingle but they may only advance to what is their highest level. In other words, a soul may mingle on a level of lower vibration but may not travel to a higher vibration beyond their own, unless they have permission and/or are escorted in the presence of a higher being.

The process is necessary for the benefit of all. No soul is eve r forced to move anywhere. Only through a period of adjustment or orientation can one begin to actualize what occurs around them.

The more work a soul can do during each incarnation, the more advancement occurs. As a soul learns during an incarnation or experience, it is as if they are pushing against a strong dense wind to progress forward.

Once in transition, the dense wind may not be present, but it takes longer to realize the truth and knowledge.

Serving others or being of service during an incarnation goes a long way in progression, both in helping to balance the scales of karma and in seeking one's own truth.

This concludes today's lesson.

Peace,

Council of 24

Today our discussion begins with opening your perimeters of expansion. Within each soul is a set of grids. The amount of development a soul chooses in a lifetime determines what gridlines are open or closed. Naturally, the higher the maturity of the soul, the more gridlines are open.

As a soul advances, more gridlines are activated. Also, we have the ability to expand the gridlines as well. This expansion will occur in those souls who have reached the completion of all necessary numbers in the matrix.

Picture a football field with chalk lines on the yards. Then, picture a touchdown run the whole length of the field. When the line in the end zone is crossed, all the chalk lines on the whole field become illuminated. Then, there was a choice to go for one extra point, or a two-point conversion. The expansion of gridlines is similar to going for a two-point conversion.

Be at peace,

Council of 24

CHAPTER 18

Good evening and many blessings of the Almighty Father be upon you.

It is of the utmost importance that you listen carefully to what we transcribe here tonight.

Today begins a new realm of energy transformation that will change the way you think, act and feel. It will begin slowly and then with time accelerate.

As a soul reaches a certain point in their journey of life, each will experience this same transference of energy. It can only occur when a soul reaches the upper echelons. This transference may be described as a universal cleansing if you will.

For some it may occur only hours, minutes or days before they make their transition.

For others, who have advanced while in body, it may happen even years before they leave the earth plane.

This universal cleansing differs for all souls. For some, it is minor, for others it may be cathartic. The soul must have done the work to achieve this.

Let us elaborate. For some souls who have done the internal healing, there may be residual energy that still lingers. This universal cleansing absorbs and releases that energy. Then the soul can work from the other side to continue their development.

In a different scenario, where a soul has completed their mission and exists within their last incarnation, a different kind of cleansing occurs. This soul has done all the work and has stepped away from the earthly mundane day to day issues of mankind. They have learned how to be of the world masses but not be in the world.

A soul must be able to exist within the masses and yet rise above to walk away from all they have known. When a soul walks away, it changes the energy dynamics for the rest of their incarnation. It changes everything, even the interactions with others.

They understand that a life of service begins with service to themselves. Until they can serve themselves, they are only fooling themselves. Serving themselves is the greatest service one can provide to the Almighty Father.

This must include forgiveness for all past acts and issues that have transpired. This must be total and complete.

One is quick to see the good in others yet can fail to see and find the good within themselves. Until a soul can truly forgive the self and can find and dwell within the good of themselves-they are being held back.

Purity and goodness of self are within. It is always there but must be felt and acknowledged by each individual soul. This is the key to peace within and a key to self-mastery.

When complete, a new awareness shall be realized.

Council of 24

CHAPTER 19

Hello again. Today we wish to examine the area of soul rescue. When a soul leaves the physical body, many areas are affected. Depending on the way in which the exit occurs, will cause different actions and results.

For a soul, whose exit is sudden, such as through an accident or at the hands of another, a great deal of confusion surrounds them. First and most often, they do not realize they have passed from their physical body. They still see and feel; therefore, they exist. The confusion magnifies when they realize they cannot be seen or heard for the most part.

Often a great deal of help is needed for them to begin to see their truth. Any unfinished business or fear only magnifies the situation. Along with this, soul maturity is involved. For an advanced soul, even if death is sudden, it takes a much shorter period for them to understand what has happened.

A soul in later years of life begins to see and plan their exit. Especially one who is content with the life that was lived; the exit will be relatively simple.

For a soul who is unsettled or feels incomplete in their journey, often the exit will be drawn out as they intuitively seek to finish and complete all they can in the time period. Once a soul begins to get near an exit point, they do an internal inventory and examine their particular journey.

Also, if a soul feels not enough is accomplished, there can be almost a panic to try and remedy various situations or experiences.

For a very advanced soul, there is merely a peace within when they realize an exit point is close. As with all souls leaving, they go through the steps in transition. However, there comes a point where the peace flows on each side of existence. They understand what is occurring, what has transpired in the lifetime, and are completely at peace on all levels. Depending on the level of numbers completed, a soul merely eases from one realm to another.

Although grief and sadness are experienced on your plane, only joy and celebration are experienced on our plane. It is important to bring peace to any matter left on your plane. Search your heart to discover what is necessary and complete what you need to do.

Take time to examine all you must to free yourself. The rewards will be many as a result.

That's all for today. Peace,

Council of 24

Good day to you. We wish to continue our discussion on soul rescue. Each soul upon exit of the physical body will find themselves in different situations. First and foremost, is their belief system. Whatever the beliefs are upon exit, give the surrounding circumstances of the soul. If the belief exists that upon death there is nothing more than darkness, then darkness will present itself for as long as necessary. There is always guidance and education available but until the soul is ready to receive such information, then only darkness will exist.

Another soul who believes that life continues will experience exactly that. Each soul in the afterlife will exist on whatever level of development that is achieved.

It is a result of misinformation presented, that upon death many souls find total confusion. They succumb to the beliefs of others, especially those in religion, rather than forming their own beliefs. Other souls who have had near death experiences, find their own beliefs instead of those of mass consciousness.

When a soul exists with the attachment to their surroundings or people, they often choose to stay in those surroundings. Tis often creates havoc for many others.

The best scenario is for a soul to be free of attachments before exiting. Then they move to the level of existence they have earned. From here they can help those still in body in many ways.

Just as there are many levels of light, there are equal numbers of levels of darkness. Again, there must be balance. Depending on the life experiences, a soul will learn and mature. Even if one has exor participated in an atrocity of events, the reason behind the atrocity must be examined. Was this predestined in order to impact and raise the mass consciousness? You must look for the good within what you consider evil.

On the other hand, one who commits evil acts repeatedly, without any remorse or concern for their actions or other souls, is an entirely different situation. They will be handled as such.

Sometimes, it takes what is thought to be a horrible event to bring the most light and higher consciousness within the realm. Picture the earth plane as a thick dense energy. Within it are millions of souls operating at a level where they do the same thing every day with their mundane lives. They are so self-absorbed that no one can get through to them. Then an event occurs, whether on a personal level or global level, that removes them from their comfort zone. Now, they can be reached. Often this is what happens.

Yet another soul will go through life doing good deeds and volunteering. However, that is about it. Again, it is all about choice. Many are predestined choices, and many are not.

For a soul to progress, they must choose to come through the darkness and into the light. There is always aid readily available; still some choose to try to do things the hard way without help.

For now, this concludes our lesson. Please think and integrate what has been discussed.

We bid you peace.

Council of 24

Once again, we are grateful for the opportunity to expand the knowledge and wisdom for all.

Each soul discovers new echelons within its course of being. As a soul nears the end of its journey of life, many new discoveries surface.

One often has an elevated awareness of all living creatures. Each day, each moment, each breath has new awareness. The unseen becomes seen, the darkness brings light.

As you enter this arena of life, your life changes moment to moment. What is cherished also changes with each moment. The mundane becomes lost as it loses its importance. Something as simple as a cloud takes on a whole new dimension. All of these changes are merely part of life's process.

When a soul has completed its journey, realization becomes a dynamic character. A great deal of reflection occurs. Time passes and through this passage many questions become answered. Often, before the questions were there lingering. Now the answers may surface. They were always there, imbedded within the soul yet, now they are realized.

The dynamics of others and their relationships are seen with the clarity of a magnifying glass. Yet, also realized is what these other souls must comprehend for themselves.

As the eye opens within the soul, elevation is experienced in a way never felt before. There is a quiet on the surface outside while a great deal of discovery occurs on the inside.

One experiences many changes within their being. Some may be unsettling as they realize the grandeur that results. Trust what is felt and seek to understand. There is a wealth of information for one to bear witness for others.

What may surface has not been experienced before. Many may challenge your words, yet many will rise to the challenge in support.

Within these words will be energy that speaks to all on many levels. Within will be peace and comfort, while removing much of the fear and replacing it with understanding.

Fear of the unknown is one of the greatest fears in existence. The gift will bring light within the darkness for all.

We bid you well.

Council of ALL

CHAPTER 20

Good day and thank you for answering this call. It is important for the paradigm of growth and development to be expanded. In doing this more clarity will prevail.

The discussion of synchronicity is one of great challenge for many souls. Often the greatest wisdom comes in silence as opposed to movement. This can be difficult to comprehend.

The universe operates only through a schedule of Universal Law. It is perfection in true form. Each soul has the opportunity to be within the flow of the universe or to be outside it. One usually knows in which direction they reside.

Picture a fluid movement of energy flowing in a straight line. Now, picture objects or boulders placed along its path. Notice that the liquid merely flows easily around each object without any disruption in flow.

Now, picture the flow of a soul's experience. Along the path are various obstacles or events that occur. The choice is there to merely flow with and around the events or react and challenge the events. When this happens, a soul deviates from the center of force and disrupts the flow. The disruption causes an imbalance of energy. Balance will be restored through Natural Law but through choice, the disruption could have been avoided.

Each thought one has will find a like-minded thought within the universe and all affect the natural flow.

Think of times when you were in your flow of life. Now, think of an event or obstacle where you chose to move within the flow and the outcome produced. Then, think of an event or obstacle where you refused to flow, reacted to the event, and created disharmony thinking it would help. What actually happened?

Remember your energy does not change, it is merely transformed. It is all about time, balance, and synchronicity.

The easiest way to maintain the flow of harmony is to simply be in the present moment. We cannot stress this enough. Forget not only the memory of the past, but the worry of the future. In doing this, you will find greater peace and harmony, both within and without your being.

We bid you good day.

Council of ALL

Good day. We continue our education of the soul. As a soul journey comes near the end, many changes take place and various scenarios may occur. For example, if a soul has endured a lengthy illness, it has major impact on their soul energy. It is greatly depleted.

For some souls, they may enter a coma. When this happens, it may seem as if they are merely asleep. In reality, a great deal is taking place. They are aware of what is going on around them and can hear whatever is said. Along with that, may guides and healers are present and working to heal and replenish their soul energy in preparation for their final departure and transition.

This soul energy differs from the energy of the physical body. It is like two separate frequencies joined as one. The healing only will occur on the soul energy. This allows for the physical energy to continue being depleted, which facilitates the transition.

The energy existing for the physical structure of the body has a much greater density in nature and components. This must occur to blend with the dense physical plane. The soul energy on the other hand is a great deal purer and refined in nature. This results from their individual level of existence in spirit world.

Picture it as if the soul energy is encased with the physical energy of the body as a protective shield. Over time the physical energy weakens through age, illness, attitudes of mental thought and many other variables. This continues for the time span of the journey.

For those who exit quickly, such as through an accident or injury, their preparation still takes place, but on a different level. That is why often these souls are confused as to what happened to them. Preparation continues when they exit their body, until and when they are willing to move forward.

For an advanced soul, the departure is much easier. They will begin their transfer of soul energy when the time is right, so their exit will be facilitated. On a conscious level, they may or may not be aware of exactly what is occurring, but they usually realize some kind of action is taking place.

We have only spoken of those who have been on the earth for a reasonable life span. In the case of a child or even an infant, the transition is handled in a different way. These individual souls are surrounded and carried by angels to their appropriate level of existence. They know no pain or discomfort and are always held in the hand of the Living god. Any pain or discomfort was only that which was experienced on the earth plane.

This concludes todays teaching. We bid you good day.

Council of ALL

CHAPTER 21

Good day to you. This is one of the few remaining discussions we wish to share. The time has come for a major shift of energy of all souls. It has great magnitude. Energies are shifting everywhere through weather patterns, wars, and destruction of many means.

The energies needed for world advancement shall be encoded within the teachings of this book. It shall impact all who read the words and along with discussions with others.

A great awakening must happen.

As a soul readies itself for the final transition, a great amount of change takes place. There are three actual exit points. Which point of exit is chosen depends on the development and level of maturity of the soul. One may exit through the lower chakras, the middle chakra, or the crown chakra. Only those of the highest maturity exit from the crown chakra. The energy would be too intense for most souls.

Each day must be cherished. Life is precious.

Council of the One

Chapter 22

Good day to you. We wish to discuss the final transcriptions of the universal teaching. We continue our discussion.

The individual soul is provided exactly what it needs for each incarnation, nothing more and nothing less. Once incarnated it is up to each individual soul to utilize what is provided from the inside.

There is a percentage of soul energy that always remains in the spirit world and other percentages of soul energies that incarnate into one or more lives. Although the percentages chosen are primarily a soul choice, there is much higher guidance involved as well.

For example, say that a soul chooses a rather uneventful lifetime. They may decide to utilize only twenty percent of their soul energy for the incarnation. The other eighty percent is shared by what remains in spirit world or also other lives may be chosen at the same time.

Now, compare this to a soul who has chosen to pay off a great deal of karma. They may decide that due to the events and experiences they must go through; they need eighty percent of their soul energy for the incarnation. The other twenty percent remains in spirit world. This twenty percent continues to grow, educate and mature.

These are both simple examples of what can transpire. There are an infinite number of scenarios that can be found in between.

A soul must assume the responsibility for their thoughts and actions. This is the basic mantra for life. Only when responsibility has been chosen can they begin to find the truth. Thus, begins the climb up the ladder of soul growth.

When a soul begins to awaken from its sleep, there is no going back. One may attempt it, but it never works. It is designed that way. Only by taking off the rose-colored glasses can one truly see. Yet it is time for all souls to come out of the dark and into the light.

May you feel the love and blessings of the universe and Almighty God the Father.

The Council of Elders

Epilogue

Everything you have learned through these teachings and meditations is truth. Each soul on their journey will go through similar steps. Some are identical, while others may vary due to soul elevation and maturity.

Within the realms of spirit world, no free will exists. Free will exists on your earth plane merely for reasons to advance one's soul growth.

Within the spirit world there exists a Divine Order. There is rule that prevails through Natural Law and balance. For many new entering souls, this can be challenging. On the other hand, for those who understand Universal Law, the transition flows like a gentle stream.

If those on earth would understand Universal Law, they would find their lives would flow much easier. Often the difficulty comes through resistance of Natural Law. The more resistance, the greater the difficulty.

Each day you are all offered opportunities which show you the flow of these laws. For many whose lives are in turmoil and whose lives did not turn out to be as they expected, it is merely due to resisting Natural Law. They knew no better because they were unaware of these laws.

However, in spirit world, all runs on Universal Law and Divine Order. Think of your day to day experience where these laws play their role. Look at the times where it flowed. Then look at the times of resistance. From each you will learn a great deal.

This ends our discussion for today.

24

This information is being offered only as a means to answer questions of those searching for truth.

For some it may be enlightening, for others it may just be confusing.

The beginning of this series of books will offer some enlightenment for all mankind. As with all things earthly, it is a choice. Do I accept these words as truth, or do I discard them as being false?

The choice is yours. Either way the energy of these words will be embedded within your being.

Whatever you choose, we are grateful for the opportunity to bring light into the darkness. Blessings to all those who read these words.

Namaste,

Council of ALL

OTHER BOOKS

Who Am I . . . Really? A Soul's Journey to Heaven